PUSH THE ROCK

Second Chances on the Road to Kilimanjaro

R W Long

Push the Rock: Second Chances on the Road to Kilimanjaro

Published in the United States by First Summit Project.
www.firstsummitproject.org

ISBN 9780996732000

ISBN: 0996732004

Library of Congress Control Number: 2015950416

First Edition

Printed in the United States of America

Cover design by R.W. Long and Lorie DeWorken
Front cover photograph by Alice and McKnight Brown
Editing by Laurie Knight
First Summit Project logo design by Jacob Cheatham

10 9 8 7 6 5 4 3 2 1

For my wife and sons:
You are my heroes and the loves of my life.

CONTENTS

FOREWORD

There is a tremendous honor when one is invited to write the foreword to a book. I know, because honor is what I felt when R.W. Long invited me to write the foreword to his book, *Push the Rock*. My first impulse was to say thanks, but no thanks. He wanted me to write the foreword? No way. That is not possible. Besides there are many other more qualified people to affirm R.W.'s work. After considering all that he had been through, however, I changed my mind. I said yes. I would write the foreword.

I have had the privilege of reading through R.W.'s drafts at least two times. As his pastor, I have also had the privilege of praying for him while he worked on this personal treasure. Each time I read a draft and prayed for him two different quotes came to mind.

The first quote originates with Martin Luther King. Dr. King was right when he said, "The ultimate measure of a man is not where he stands in moments of comfort and convenience, but where he stands in times of challenge and controversy." R.W. Long is a living witness to King's maxim.

R.W. once had it all. In short, he was living the American Dream. Then it all came crashing down. His fall was hard, brutally hard. Many would have never jumped back to their feet, but not R.W. Even though the challenges are more stressful and painful today, he stands taller than he ever did before.

The second quote is not as easy to credit. Yet it is equally effective. It has been said by more than a few people, "You will be the same person you are today except for the people you meet and the books you read." In short, books and people matter. They matter because they influence you.

You may never meet R.W. Long, but you can certainly read his book. And by reading his book, your life will be different. You will be challenged and inspired. You will be jolted and stimulated. You may even be forced to change the course of your own life.

I am not only R.W.'s pastor I am also his friend. So it is for that reason I heartily recommend to you *Push the Rock*. As his friend I know his struggles. I also know his joys. We should be thankful he has labored to share those struggles and joys with us.

Be careful as you read *Push the Rock*, however. Be careful because it will change you. You will be jolted from your seat. You may even be rocked out of your comfort zone.

May 2015
Dr. Ryan F. Whitley
Founding and Senior Pastor
CrossPoint Church
Trussville, Alabama

AUTHOR'S NOTE

There are no composite characters or events in this book. I have tried to recreate events, locales, and conversations from my memories of them. In order to maintain their anonymity in some instances I have changed the names of individuals, and I may have changed some identifying characteristics and details. Basic information presented in the book about Parkinson's disease symptoms and treatments is readily available from neurologists, movement disorders specialists, and organizations such as The Michael J. Fox Foundation for Parkinson's Research (MJFF), the Parkinson's Disease Foundation (PDF), the National Parkinson Foundation (NPF), and the Davis Phinney Foundation (DPF).

PROLOGUE

There, ahead, all he could see, as wide as all the world
great, high, and unbelievably white in the sun,
was the square top of Kilimanjaro.
And then he knew that there was where he was going.

ERNEST HEMINGWAY

Between the shadows of camp and the brilliant night sky, the pitch black consumed most of my vision. I had many images of the flat-topped peak stored in my mind, but seeing the mountain in silhouette seemed to amplify its vastness.

The cloud cover that had enveloped the camp upon our arrival just a few hours earlier was gone, replaced by a crystal clear night sky above Kilimanjaro. At just after midnight, the stars were dazzling. The sky was free from the refracted glow of civilization that blinds us from seeing the bright natural pinpoints of light against unsullied blackness. It reminded me of the Sky Theater at the Adler Planetarium in Chicago, but this was the real show, not something recreated by man.

Well above the last remnants of plant life on the mountain, Barafu Camp sits on a ridge overlooking the Karanga Valley a few kilometers west of the mountain's second highest summit, Mawenzi. Completely exposed to the elements at 15,300 feet above sea level, it is the last vestige of civilization before the final ascent to the summit. Barafu means "ice" in Swahili, and the name is fitting. More a pit stop than a rest stop for those on their way to the summit, climbers spend only a short time at the camp for a meal and a few hours of sleep before continuing on.

Climbers from several routes converge on this bare and frigid camp before making the daunting push to Uhuru Peak, the highest summit on Mt. Kilimanjaro and the highest point on the African continent. Guides tell climbers that a nighttime ascent is best to experience sunrise on the summit—of which there is no argument—but there is certainly an ulterior motive. If climbers could see the steep, seemingly unending uphill grade before them during the final ascent, perhaps many would give up and turn back well before reaching the peak.

The light from the oval moon revealed just enough of the barren landscape to see the rough outline of the camp, the smooth curves of tents juxtaposed against the jagged edges of the rocky terrain. I stood in the moonlit darkness looking uphill at my destiny. Inhaling deeply, I forced the thin, cold air into my lungs to ready myself for the task before me. The twinkling of the headlamps of the climbers who had left camp earlier formed a line beginning at the edge of camp, fairly flat at first then changing direction abruptly. The nearly ninety-degree bend in the line of headlamps marked the beginning of the trek up the steep volcanic cone that seemed so far away.

I had known for several months that the moon would be in the waxing gibbous phase on this night. I also knew that awareness of such detail bordered on the fanatical. The moon would provide just enough ambient light to see little more than a few steps in front of me should my headlamp fail. It appeared to be much larger than normal at nearly three miles above sea level.

Once roused from the brink of fitful sleep, thirty minutes were needed for the members of our group to make nearly frozen limbs perform their duties, wriggle free of our tents, check our packs, and test our gear for readiness. Throughout this exercise, our guides waited patiently in a group while chatting in Swahili, their backs against the cold descending from Kibo, the youngest, highest, and most recognizable of the three volcanic cones on Kilimanjaro. One by one we deemed ourselves as ready as we could be for the night ahead and assembled in a tight group. Only then did we learn that our number would be reduced by one because of illness. I had suspected as much, but it was disheartening nonetheless.

Each of us wanted the other members of the group to make it to the summit, but in that moment I understood the success of each climber would be determined by the ability to delve into the solitude of one's soul and find the strength to overcome the body's resistance every step of the way. Although physical fitness and adrenaline had brought us this far, tenacity and mental endurance would be the keys to success in reaching the summit.

The quiet of the night was broken by Steven, the lead Tanzanian guide. With the calm, upbeat voice we had become accustomed to, he asked a question. He spoke in Swahili. "*Twende?*" (Are we ready to go?)

In unison our group replied affirmatively, likewise in Swahili. "*Sawa sawa!*" (Okay!)

We began moving quietly and slowly through the shadows of the camp to the starting point for the final ascent, our goal to reach the summit at sunrise. As we left high camp behind us, I felt a mixture of emotions, but most of all, I was resolute. I went forward into the darkness not knowing if I would reach freedom by daylight, but I did know I would give my all in the effort. The decade-long fight for my life had prepared me well for this night.

1

THE STORM

Hardship often prepares an ordinary person
for an extraordinary destiny.

C.S. LEWIS

Moving forward into the darkness isn't new to me. It had been the theme of the previous decade of my life before my time on Kilimanjaro. Life is always filled with uncertainty, but we convince ourselves otherwise with our five or ten year plans, believing we can see into the future and that our paths are well-lit by our own brilliance. We acquire things, mark items off checklists, accomplish goals on time or ahead of schedule, and think we are in control of our lives. We believe that we are the captains of our ships and that our accomplishments and possessions give us worth and define who we are. It was the lie I lived for the first thirty-six years of my life.

As soon as my feet touched the floor and my legs failed me for the first time, I knew the life I had built was about to change and quite possibly slip from my grasp. It wasn't a conscious thought, rather a deep, instinctual knowledge of a new reality. It took years to learn how to navigate through the storm that followed, yet it was the storm that showed me who I really am, who God is, and the life I am meant to live. It tested me, broke me, revealed many truths to me, and eventually shaped me into the person I was destined to be all along.

Halloween of 2002 was the last normal day of my life, one that still held all the hopes and expectations of someone who has experienced mostly smooth sailing, someone who has yet to see his first major storm of adulthood. Although I now know that a part of my brain has been dying since my twenties, I only became aware of the storm when I awoke the following morning and discovered that my left leg refused to follow the commands my brain was sending. That miscommunication between my brain and body was the first bolt of lightning and crack of thunder heralding the dark skies ahead.

I thought I had injured myself during a recent workout and was seeing a delayed result. Oddly, I felt no pain. My leg just wouldn't do what my brain was telling it to do. I skipped the gym to see if the problem would get better. My coworkers, my buddies, gave me grief all week. I laughed with them because I knew how odd my new walk looked. *Step-drag, step-drag.* I tried to put off seeing a doctor as long as possible because I hated going. I didn't like to be around sick people, especially cooped up in a small physician's waiting room. I was strong as a bull, more prone to injuries from playing or working than to illness.

A week after the first sign of "the problem," I stood beside my bed at four in the morning trying to make my legs move, but they were glued to the floor. Several minutes passed before the first sign of movement. Although I still couldn't lift my feet, I was able to shuffle across the bedroom floor to the bathroom. Once there, I sat on the side of the bathtub for a few minutes trying to make sense of what was happening. I was bewildered, but I didn't panic. My lifelong friend, logic, went to work without prodding, assessing the situation. What had started out as a nuisance a week earlier had suddenly become a significant problem.

For the first time of many to come, I called out to my wife for help. Olivia, or Liv for short, arose in a groggy stupor and helped me dress for work. I didn't want her to worry, so I told her I probably had injured a nerve in my back working out and it was getting worse before getting better. She'd seen me be injured or wounded, cut and scraped, and bumped and bruised from work and from play, but this was different.

I made it to work and through the day, giving the same excuses to my coworkers. I heard "you're just getting old" or "this is what happens when you try to do the stuff you did when you were younger" all day from my coworkers. Again, I laughed with them, but my mind worked problem solving exercises throughout the day, assessing cause and effect. No answers came.

When I arrived home, I avoided letting my sons see how difficult it was for me to walk. At thirteen and nine years old, they were busy playing video games or sandlot sports with each other and friends. I was one of the least interesting people in their lives, so it wasn't difficult to hide my condition from them that night.

Luckily, I would have the weekend to see if my condition would improve. With a full slate of college and pro football, the highlight of which would be watching my alma mater, the University of Tennessee, take on the University of Miami Hurricanes, the number one ranked football team in the nation. I would have the perfect excuse to camp out on the couch and forget about my problem for a few hours.

As I lay in bed that night, I told myself that I had overreacted that morning when I thought my life was going to change. Again, I was caught up in the lie: that I was in control, that I alone determined the course my life would follow. I would soon learn just how wrong I was, and discover the truth of the Proverb, *"The heart of man plans his way; but the Lord establishes his steps"* (Proverbs 16:9 English Standard Version).

Balance soon became an issue. Instinctively, I reached out to touch the closest wall to steady myself at home. Walking in public was an adventure, and I became self-conscious quickly as I drew stares from others who must have wondered if I was intoxicated. Within a few weeks, I had to buy a cane to help me walk. It seemed an odd purchase for someone my age to make, and I didn't know where to shop for one. I settled on an adjustable, collapsible cane I found in a well-hidden display in a chain pharmacy, and was surprised by how quickly I became dependent on the aluminum stick with a wooden handle.

The boys eventually noticed something wasn't quite right, and when I didn't improve they became concerned. I lied to them, telling them that it would take some time for my back to heal. Outwardly, I carried on with my life as if a problem didn't exist. Inside, I was angry and frustrated. I was angry that I couldn't make my legs do what I wanted them to do and humbled when I had to ask coworkers for help to fulfill some of my job duties. I was frustrated with my primary care physician because, after conducting several tests, he had no answers and seemed evasive when pressed.

During the Christmas season, new symptoms developed. My left arm became rigid and nearly useless and I noticed it didn't swing when I walked. I wasn't sure if the lack of arm swing was a new development or not. Then the bobble head (head/neck tremor) started. It was at this point when Liv finally voiced the concerns she had kept to herself, and suggested that I had been covering up the severity of the problem.

Random coworkers asked me what was wrong, to which I would reply, "MS, ALS, Parkinson's, brain tumor—take your pick at this point," in a sick attempt at humor. I had no answers, so I just made fun of my situation. I thought humor was the best course of action, primarily to put others at ease, but also because I didn't like to hear people complain about their problems. Mostly, I was too proud to admit that I was scared.

Having reached the limits of his capabilities, including what seemed like every blood test known to man and an MRI of my spine, my primary care physician finally referred me to a well-known neurologist in Birmingham. I never saw the primary physician again. Looking back, I realize how crazy it was to lay in an MRI machine thinking my best case scenario was surgery on my spine to fix what I hoped was just a mechanical problem. *Yo, Doc, please cut me open and tinker with my spine while risking paralysis. Just fix the problem.* The thought seemed logical at the time.

In the interim, I decided to do my own research. Based on my symptoms, it didn't take long to narrow the list of possibilities to Parkinson's disease. The more I read the more it made sense, but I refused to believe it for a couple of reasons. First, I had always been averse to seeing or hearing people self-diagnose. Second, I was only thirty-six years old. Fewer than 10% of people diagnosed with Parkinson's disease are younger than fifty, so the odds that I didn't have Parkinson's appeared to be in my favor.

I thought I had reached the max level of frustration through my dealings with my former primary care physician, but I was mistaken. The appointment with the neurologist did not go well at all. His arrogance was like an aura that surrounded him, and his lack of interest and ineptitude by default clashed with my determination to find the answers I was desperately seeking.

Upon reflection, I understand at that point I was far from being considered a model patient. Upon entering the bowels of the health care system, far too many people give up their individual voices and become like mindless sheep because they believe they have no other option than to blindly trust physicians. It's not like I *wanted* him to tell me that I had an incurable disease. I just needed answers, not bluster from an arrogant physician.

Although I didn't get any answers that day, I did leave the neurologist's office with an appointment to see a motion disorders specialist (a neurologist who has received exceptionally specialized training) at the Kirklin Clinic, an outpatient super clinic that is part of the University of Alabama at Birmingham Health System. People in the area refer to it as the "Cleveland Clinic of the South." I had come up empty-handed so far, but I had renewed hope that I would find an answer at the Kirklin Clinic.

Several weeks passed waiting for the appointment, and 2002 ended with no answers. A few days before the appointment with the motion disorders specialist at Kirklin, my condition suddenly worsened. My public outing happened while at work in the middle of a team meeting attended by dozens of coworkers. Up until that point, only those who worked closely with me suspected something serious was going on. Any chance I had of dealing with the severity of my condition in relative privacy evaporated that day.

The head and neck tremor became so violent that it made it difficult to breathe. My manager and close friend, Jake, ended the meeting prematurely and called Liv at the hospital where she worked. She made him promise to see that I made it to the emergency room a few floors down from her office as soon as possible. I refused his offer to drive me to Birmingham, and I barely made it to the emergency room on my own. When he saw me a few days later, Jake made it clear that he wasn't happy with me or my stubbornly stupid decision.

Liv briefed the ER doctor regarding the history of my condition, the tests that had been performed, and the physicians I had seen. Without hesitation, the young ER doctor asked me if I wanted to try some Parkinson's medication to see if I could get some relief from the symptoms. Since I couldn't speak and couldn't control the involuntarily shaking of my head in up and down, side to side motions, I gave him a simple thumbs up sign. I took the medication and promptly fell asleep. When I woke an hour later, the symptoms had subsided a bit. I was unsure if it was the result of the sleep or the medication.

I slept a lot over the weekend and took the medication the ER doctor had sent home with Liv. It was the first time I felt any relief in months. We knew what I was facing even before the appointment with the motion disorders specialist. After all of the doctor appointments, tests, and lack of information, it had taken a trip to the emergency room to find the answers we had been desperately seeking. The appointment with the motion disorders specialist would likely be anticlimactic.

Based on my recent experiences, Liv and I went into the appointment at the Kirklin Clinic expecting an adversarial relationship with yet another physician. It couldn't have been further from the truth. I have never encountered a physician who is more of a patient advocate than Dr. Nicholas. Liv and I spent two hours with Dr. Nicholas that day in January 2003. His physical examination was extremely thorough, but what he really excelled at was listening. He asked pertinent questions and listened attentively as we described the history of my symptoms in detail.

There are no definitive blood or lab tests to help a physician diagnose Parkinson's disease. Most tests are performed to rule out other diseases that may be causing symptoms. Based on the tests that had been performed, we knew I didn't have MS or a brain tumor. To diagnose Parkinson's, a specialist conducts a neurological exam, including watching a patient walk, and performing other movement, strength, and balance tests. A physician may try medication to see if an effect on symptoms occurs. In most cases, if the medication works the patient is diagnosed with Parkinson's disease. Depending on age, the diagnosis may become more specific (e.g., Young Onset Parkinson's disease).

According to the Parkinson's Disease Foundation, "Parkinson's involves the malfunction and death of vital nerve cells in the brain, called neurons. Parkinson's primarily affects neurons in an area of the brain called the substantia nigra. Some of these dying neurons produce dopamine, a chemical that sends messages to the part of the brain that controls movement and coordination. As PD progresses, the amount of dopamine produced in the brain decreases, leaving a person unable to control movement normally. The specific group of symptoms that an individual experiences varies from person to person. Primary motor signs of Parkinson's disease include the following: tremor of the hands, arms, legs, jaw and face; bradykinesia or slowness of movement; rigidity or stiffness of the limbs and trunk; and postural instability or impaired balance and coordination" (Parkinson's Disease Foundation, 2015).

When all of Dr. Nicholas's questions had been asked and answered by us, he said, "I have good news and bad news." Without asking us which news we wanted first, he told us the bad news was he knew the enemy we were facing. He was certain I had a movement disorder, leading him to believe that I had Young Onset Parkinson's disease. However, he wanted to observe the progression of my symptoms over the course of the next several months before making a formal diagnosis.

The average age of onset of Parkinson's is 62 years of age. Patients who are diagnosed below the age of 50 are typically diagnosed with Young Onset Parkinson's disease, with approximately 10% of Parkinson's cases diagnosed below an age of 40.3 years (National Parkinson Foundation, 2015). At the time of diagnosis, I was more than two decades younger than the average age of onset, which makes me one of the unlucky 10%. Per Dr. Nicholas, the good news was that we could make decisions based on having the answer and could proceed with treatment and get on with our lives. Although he was well-intentioned, it was if he had placed a noose around my neck then told me I could go merrily on my way.

When I asked Dr. Nicholas why the other doctors I had seen didn't have any answers, he replied matter-of-factly that his specialized training and experience with motion disorders, specifically Parkinson's disease, enabled him to make diagnoses with a high degree of certainty. He explained further that he considered my symptoms to be somewhat atypical. The absence of hand tremor and the suddenness with which my symptoms developed could easily lead to an incorrect or a non-diagnosis by lesser trained physicians.

Parkinson's disease manifests as a different disease for each individual. For example, assume there are ten classic symptoms associated with Parkinson's. If each symptom was written on a small piece of paper and put into a paper bag then a person reaches into the bag and grabs a handful, each person would have a slightly different set of symptoms written on pieces of paper. Each person with Parkinson's has a different version of the disease with varying symptoms, varying degrees of the speed of progression, severity of symptoms, and responses to treatment. One person may need medication to be able to move at all while another may be able to function fairly well for some time before needing medication.

In essence, Parkinson's is an individual disease with varying presentations that is categorized as one. This concept was something I wasn't able to grasp at the time of diagnosis, and it would take quite some time before I would fully understand the individuality of the disease.

Dr. Nicholas's confidence put me at ease. I took it as a man supremely confident in his training and intelligence. The primary difference between Dr. Nicholas and the other physicians I had seen was that he seemed to be as genuinely interested in finding answers as we were. He and I just clicked. I knew he would be my champion and my guide through what was to come.

At that point in our lives, just having an answer was a relief. Not knowing what was wrong with me had driven me nearly insane. Having *the* answer didn't scare us too badly. Liv and I had come through some tough times growing up as kids from broken, blue collar families, and later when we were barely adult newlyweds and parents. We considered ourselves to be tougher than most people based on our life experiences. More importantly, it didn't scare us because of our faith in God. We believed He had a reason for allowing this to happen to me.

Although His purpose was not evident at the time, we still believed. Looking back, I'm thankful for our ignorance regarding the challenges Parkinson's disease would present and the blissful naiveté that accompanied our faith. Had we known in that moment the obstacles, challenges, and near complete upheaval in our lives that lay ahead of us, we would have been scared out of our minds.

2

KILIMANJARO: DAYBREAK IN AFRICA

23 AUG 2012

Since the beginning of my new life, I wake at daybreak without prompting, excited to see what the day holds. I was the first one up in our hotel room, which had been hurriedly prepared by hotel staff to simulate a dorm room for the three oldest members of the group.

My first look at Africa in the daylight came through an open fifth floor window of The Impala Hotel in Arusha. The city was already bustling at this early hour. The streets were packed with vehicle traffic and many more bicycles than I was accustomed to seeing at home, even in a bicycling-crazy state like Colorado. Beyond the boundary of the lush hotel property and the busy streets beyond was a school with a barren soccer field, billboards in Swahili advertising cell phone providers or soft drinks, and small houses that stood out among unfamiliar vegetation and trees. Childlike, I was mesmerized by every sight, sound, and smell.

I had lived and breathed and thought of little other than Africa for the past seven months, and I was eager to get out into the city to see the sights during our one free day before beginning the six-day journey on Kilimanjaro. Every moment of this day held something new, and I felt like a kid at Christmas, ready to wake everyone in the house. When I looked at Brad and Dan, my new teammates, still deep asleep underneath the mosquito netting surrounding their beds and unaffected by the daylight now filling the room, I decided to spare them my excitement for a while longer.

I was grateful that I wasn't symptomatic following the long trip from the United States. The flights from Denver to Detroit to Amsterdam to Kilimanjaro International near Moshi had taken approximately twenty hours. The part of the trip from the United States to Amsterdam had been the typical torture chamber of babies and small children crying, people talking loudly, and the restlessness that accompanies settling in for such a long trip. I tried to ignore them by focusing on the little airplane icon as it crept along the arc of the flight path over the Atlantic on the seatback monitor in front of me.

I had met Dan in the Detroit airport and most of the rest of the group for the first time during the layover in Amsterdam, which felt like the true beginning of the adventure. These were my teammates, the people with whom I would share the climb on Kilimanjaro. The part of the trip from Amsterdam to Tanzania was much more tolerable than the first leg. The majority of passengers were destined for Mt. Kilimanjaro and most of the remaining passengers were likely booked on Serengeti safaris of various lengths. There must have been enough hiking clothing and gear aboard the flight to stock a small REI store.

We arrived after nightfall, so rather than Mt. Kilimanjaro dominating the horizon, our first sight in Africa was a dark tarmac and a small, flat, square building. Taking in the sights was the least of our concerns, though, as passengers were hustled from the plane into the crowded terminal, which seemed much too small to accommodate the full flight disembarking from KLM's Airbus.

My teammates and I were anxious about completing the immigration forms for a Tanzanian visa, ensuring cash was in hand for the application fee, but most importantly, that our bags had arrived at the airport with us. If my extra-large base camp duffel didn't appear on the baggage carousel, I would be in big trouble. Everything in my bag was necessary for the climb. I had painstakingly planned for the trek, and didn't want to be the guy who wore the same clothes every day of the climb, begging and borrowing items from teammates.

The visa application process went much easier than expected. The immigration officer didn't bother to look at the forms I had meticulously completed in my best block lettering. Instead, she snatched the forms and the C-note from my hand, stamped and wrote in my passport, and pointed to the baggage claim area. The baggage claim process went smoothly with no bags missing in action.

With the apprehension of making it through immigration and baggage claim behind us, we stepped through the doors to the airport reception area and were immediately bombarded by a crowd of locals shouting and holding hand-made placards with names on them waiting to accompany their passengers to buses or taxis. Fortunately, Will, the leader of our group, had arrived in Tanzania several days prior for a warm-up climb of Mt. Meru, and was waiting to welcome us. It was great to finally lay eyes on and shake the hand of the young man with whom I had communicated for several months. Within minutes, our bags were loaded on the old Toyota bus and we were hurtling through the darkness on what my brain screamed was the wrong side of the road. Excited chatter filled the bus, each of us feeling a brief reprieve from the long, tiring series of flights. *I'm actually here. I'm in Africa!* was on repeat in my mind, even as I took part in multiple conversations during the hour-long ride from Kilimanjaro International to the hotel in Arusha. After checking in and enjoying a rowdy midnight dinner as a group, everyone retreated to their rooms, closed the mosquito netting around his/her bed, and slept like the dead. Everyone, I assume, except me.

Even though my body was exhausted, my mind was working overtime. For what seemed like hours, I tried to turn it off and go to sleep to no avail. Somewhere in the night, as thoughts precipitated in my mind about the unlikely road that had brought me to this point in my life—to Tanzania to climb the tallest mountain in Africa—sleep finally came for me.

3

BEFORE THE STORM

*I was born for the storm,
and a calm does not suit me.*

ANDREW JACKSON

My life up until I was sucker-punched by Parkinson's disease had been about building my own version of the American Dream typically depicted in Norman Rockwell paintings. I'm the oldest of three boys, and our dad left us and our mother when I was fourteen to live the rest of his life bouncing between bottles of cheap Kentucky bourbon and VA hospitals. I didn't mind because he had been my tormenter for as long as I could remember.

My mom worked multiple jobs to provide for her sons. I took on even more of a leadership role for my younger brothers' sake and to lessen the burden my mom bore. She has always been my hero for sacrificing most of her youthful dreams and aspirations to ensure that my brothers and I were provided with the basics we needed, but more importantly, for giving us the love and support essential for becoming men.

With the loss of my father's income, times were tough financially, so I started working at a younger age than most. I mowed grass, baled and stacked hay, raked leaves, painted houses, and took any other odd jobs I could find throughout the eastern part of Tennessee. Playing football was my saving grace. As a teen, I lived to play the sport. To do so, I had to keep my grades up. And with the additional demands of working odd jobs to help my mom and younger brothers and provide for myself, I had little time to get into the troubles often associated with the teen years.

My football days ended with my graduation from high school, but the hard work in the classroom paid off with an academic scholarship to the local community college. Three years later with a couple Associate of Science degrees on the wall, I began my professional career at a federal research facility near my hometown.

I met Liv not long after my career began. She was a beautiful, blond-haired, green-eyed, free-spirited recent high school graduate. She had been a freshman when I was a senior at the same high school, but our paths had never crossed. She lived with her mom and they were my upstairs neighbors in the apartment complex where I had my first home as an adult. We had been secretly admiring each other from afar for several months, but neither of us had initiated contact. The chemistry was evident, even before we spoke our first words to each other. The attraction felt like a coming lightning strike.

During the third weekend of June 1987, in a sleepy little lake town in Tennessee, I went for a drive to see what kind of mischief I could find. When I fired up the engine and pulled out onto the road, I couldn't have known I would finally meet the one who would become my wife, my best friend, the mother of the children we would one day have, and my partner in life from that day forward. It all started when I spotted the feisty young beauty I had a secret crush on, hanging out with her friends at the lakeside city park. I could resist no longer, and asked if she wanted to take a ride around town. The trajectory of both our lives changed when she said yes.

Not long into our relationship, we knew we wanted to be married and wasted little time on a long engagement, eloping late one February night to a small wedding chapel in Gatlinburg, Tennessee. We kept the elopement secret much to our own amusement, and had a formal church wedding in our home town a few months later. Since the beginning, we celebrate both wedding anniversaries each year.

I promised Liv that I would love her for the rest of my life, work hard, always provide for her, and someday I would buy her a dream house complete with a white picket fence if it was what she wanted. She believed in me and my dreams, and it meant the world to me. I was fascinated by everything about her. Fourteen months after we eloped, we became the parents of a beautiful, healthy baby boy. Instinctively, we knew he was a "he" well before the doctor confirmed his gender. Eli rocked our world.

Barely into our twenties and married for little more than a year, Liv and I were the first of our group of friends to become parents, just as we had been among the first to be married. As is the case with most firstborn children and grandchildren, it seemed the sun rose and set on his face. Liv and I were destined to be parents—Eli's parents. We reveled in everything he did, every pound he gained, every inch he grew, and every sound he made. His presence added fuel to our love for each other and gave us purpose every minute of the day. We were head over heels in love with him. He was the source of our happiness, and losing him became our greatest fear.

She had fallen in love with Eli while still in the womb, constantly talking to him, telling him how much he was loved. Although overwhelmed at times being a young, first-time mother, Liv was born to be a mom. When I arrived home from work, she delighted in giving me a rundown of everything he did throughout the day. Five weeks into his young life, we faced our first encounter with possibly losing him. Eli developed a rare condition that required emergency surgery.

Our extended family arrived at the children's hospital just as Eli was taken into surgery. We realized how tiny our world had become while in the surgery waiting room. We sat there in a stupor barely noticing the events playing out on the television, the news reports and images of the protests in Tiananmen Square that would result in the Tiananmen Square Massacre a little more than a week later.

Our world had become Eli. For us, history was marked by events in his life rather than world events that become the common knowledge chronicled in history books. When the surgeon came out of the operating room, he told us that the surgery had gone well and Eli would make a full recovery. We could finally exhale. We couldn't have known that years later, another devastating world event would impact Eli's life in such a way that would make this emergency seem small and distant.

Within the first five years after graduation from high school, I completed a portion of my education, started my professional career, married, and had become a parent. The foundation of our American Dream had been laid, and the structure was going up quickly. The canvas of our Norman Rockwell painting had been framed and the outlines were drawn. It depicted two young lovers looking at each other from across a small dining table and a baby asleep in his high chair, a single candle lighting the small room in their home.

Our lives didn't slow down. I worked full time and was a full-time college student in addition to being a husband and father. Within a few months of completing my education, we moved to north Texas, where Max was born. We were blessed with a second beautiful and healthy son. Once again we experienced the joy of a new child, relishing every moment with him. The canvas of our lives expanded to include a larger table in a larger room with four characters now in place, and the paint on canvas was beginning to dry.

For the remainder of my twenties and early thirties we relocated several times to other parts of the country as my career progressed, eventually returning to Tennessee. When the boys were younger, relocating didn't seem to matter that much to them. They made friends quickly and thought of the moves as adventures. We enjoyed living in Tennessee again, and the boys were comfortable with their place in life. They liked their schools, their friends, and their ball teams. Liv's career was just beginning to take off and was in high demand, easily transportable to just about any location in the country. When the opportunity came for a destination job with a multi-national company, it was a difficult decision to move one more time. Although we weren't necessarily excited about living in Alabama at that point, the opportunity to work for a well-known automaker starting up a new plant near Birmingham was too good to pass up.

After the move, I worked long hours during the plant startup followed by the beginning of production in late 2001, but I enjoyed my job and my coworkers. The opportunities it provided for our family were incredible. In the spring of 2002, fourteen years after I promised Liv I would buy her dream house someday, we stepped into the house that would become our new home. It felt like a castle, our castle.

Two kids from single-parent, blue collar families had come so far together. All the hard work, the long hours in college classes, the moves around the country, and the bumps in the road along the way had led us to this sweet spot in life. We were incredibly happy with each other, our kids, our jobs, and our new home.

There was no way we could have known the pinnacle of life we were enjoying was actually located in the eye of a hurricane. There was no warning of the destructive storm that would move through our lives. Less than a year after moving into our dream house, I was given a life sentence and incarcerated in a prison from which there was no known escape—a body that I no longer had control over, a body that would fail me in new ways daily.

4

BACK TO THE FUTURE PAST

Life is good, and there's no reason to think it won't be—
right up until the moment when everything explodes
into a fireball of tiny, unrecognizable fragments,
or it all goes skidding sideways, through the guardrail,
over the embankment, and down the mountain.

MICHAEL J. FOX

*P*rogressive. *Degenerative. No cure.* I had thought of Parkinson's as a disease that primarily strikes older people. Liv and I read all of the material Dr. Nicholas had given us, and researched every reputable website we could find to gain a basic knowledge of the disease and its prognosis. We soon realized that our knowledge of Parkinson's disease couldn't even scratch the surface of the tip of an iceberg.

We armed ourselves with more information than we could comprehend, but had no idea how to proceed from a practical standpoint. To say the information was depressing is an understatement. Boiled down, all of it seemed to say, "Enjoy today, because tomorrow will be difficult, and every day for the remainder of your life will be harder than the one before it." We desperately needed a mentor, someone who had experienced living with the disease, but I had never met anyone who had Parkinson's disease from whom I could seek counsel. Eventually, I found him in a bookstore, and boy, did he look familiar.

In the summer of 1985, I was a college sophomore working two part-time jobs. My days started early with the dreaded eight a.m. classes, and ended late at night after arriving home from work, followed by two hours of studying for my classes. It was a lot of work and stress for a nineteen year-old and I had few outlets, one of which was going to see the most recent movie release on Saturday nights.

During one weekend in July, I went with a group of friends to see the newest hit movie, *Back to the Future*. I thought Michael J. Fox was great in the lead role. I also thought he was one lucky guy to be so young, yet to have so much success. The movie and time spent with my friends was an enjoyable, memorable respite from my hectic life. As I moved on with the grinding cycle of school-work-study-sleep-a-few-hours days and weeks, I had no idea that eighteen years later the young actor in the *Back to the Future* movie I saw on a summer Saturday night while still a teenager would play such a pivotal role in my life.

As an occasional viewer of the *Family Ties* and *Spin City* television series and a fan of the *Back to the Future* movies, I was as surprised as most when Michael J. Fox made his Parkinson's diagnosis known to the world. Liv and I had watched stories about him on some human interest and news shows and thought he must be tough and brave in real life, traits I had never before attributed to a comedic actor. He didn't complain about his condition. He seemed to just soldier on in the face of adversity. He even started a foundation to fund research to find the cure.

Apart from Muhammad Ali, he was the most famous person in the world who was fighting Parkinson's disease. He was just a few years older than I, but had been dealing with the disease in private for several years. Much to my benefit he had written about his experience, and his book, *Lucky Man*, was new on book store shelves. I discovered that although we led extremely different lives, we shared something in common that radically changed our lives in much the same manner. Without having met him in person, Michael J. Fox became my newest mentor.

5

KILIMANJARO: THE STREETS
OF ARUSHA

23 AUG 2012

The concierge's name was Mr. Anderson. None of us believed his real name was Mr. Anderson, because many of the Tanzanians who work in the tourism industry adopt names similar to their guests or customers to make it easier for everyone involved. If our group had been from Europe, he easily could have been Mr. Schmidt or Mr. Martin. He wore a crisp, dark green, short-sleeved uniform that didn't look like a uniform.

As we mingled in the hotel lobby, some of my teammates and I said his name like Agent Smith pronounced Neo's real surname in the *Matrix* movie trilogy. Mr. Anderson didn't get the joke, but he didn't seem to mind. He gave us placating smiles while going about the business of coordinating the movement of guests' baggage and giving directions to other hotel staff.

One by one the members of our group who had arrived the night before assembled in the lobby of The Impala for our excursion into Arusha. The few remaining stragglers were scheduled to arrive at various times throughout the day. Once the members of our group were present and accounted for, Mr. Anderson led us into a world much different from the one we had known just forty-eight hours earlier.

I had thought riding in a bus on the left side of the road was disorienting, but it paled in comparison to navigating the city traffic. Crossing streets and walking on the sidewalks of Arusha may entail much more risk than climbing Mt. Kilimanjaro. The city was a mind-jarring explosion of activity and culture. Everything was so new and different from anything I had ever experienced.

It didn't take long for our large group of Mzungu to be swarmed by street vendors selling beautiful art on canvas scrolls, hand-made bracelets, and an assortment of trinkets. *Mzungu* is the term many Tanzanians use for people of foreign descent. First used to describe European explorers in the eighteenth century, its literal meaning is "someone who wanders aimlessly." The European explorers traveled from one village to the next on foot, carrying their possessions in the baggage of that era, talking to the villagers along the way to get a feel for the country they were exploring.

The apparent lack of a destination or specific purpose for traveling from one village to the next led the people of Tanzania and other East African countries to think the fair-skinned strangers were wandering aimlessly. Over time the term *Mzungu* has morphed into one used for anyone with white skin. The literal meaning, one who wanders aimlessly, was once fitting for me. I had been a Mzungu for the majority of the last decade, but no more.

The street vendors definitely understood the art of the hustle. Divide and conquer. They were pleasant, chatty, and quite persistent. They wanted their targets, usually at the tail end of the group, to stop walking long enough to hear their sales pitch. While leading the group through the streets, Mr. Anderson circled back, spoke briefly to the street vendors, and then we resumed our trek to the next destination. It appeared that Mr. Anderson was well known on the streets of Arusha near The Impala, and was not one to be crossed. It was impressive.

Our group spent a few hours marveling at the craftsmanship of the artists' works at a co-op and an open air market. Although I had resolved to forego buying anything before the climb because any items would eventually end up in my duffel to be carried up and down Kilimanjaro by the porters, I couldn't pass up a couple small, frameless oil paintings on canvas depicting Kilimanjaro's peak and the Maasai people. I really wanted the paintings, but it was the earnest sales pitch of and pleasant interaction with a young Tanzanian that sealed the deal.

After lunch in the open air courtyard of a restaurant and some more sightseeing, we returned to the hotel for a few hours of downtime before meeting again for dinner. Although it's easy to see the nearly 15,000-foot peak of Mt. Meru from everywhere in Arusha, I was disappointed because I had been in Tanzania for almost twenty-four hours and hadn't seen the mountain I came to Africa to climb. I was ready to get on with it.

Will got word to everyone in the group to meet in the lobby before dinner. Once our group assembled, he led us to the rooftop of the hotel. We weaved our way around cables, satellite dishes, piping, and other facility hardware, unsure if we were allowed to be in this part of the hotel. We were unaware of what we were doing up on the roof, but I hoped we had Mr. Anderson's blessing. After seeing him in action earlier in the day, I didn't want to be in the man's dog house.

Mt. Meru dominated our view, and from this vantage point we could see much of Arusha. Daylight was waning as dusk began closing in on us. Will pointed toward the horizon. Approximately fifty miles to the northeast we could see the faint outline of Mt. Kilimanjaro in the distance. Not much was said for several minutes as the members of our group stood there looking at our destination. Even at this distance, I could see how the mountain dominated the plains of Africa. It was massive.

Two additional members of our group arrived while we were on the roof. They had come from another part of Africa, where they had been on safari to celebrate their first wedding anniversary. The final two members of our group arrived from New York during our dinner gathering. Our group was now complete. All sixteen members had arrived safely in Tanzania. Introductions were made all around and we enjoyed the last normal dinner meal we would have for a week. Afterward, we returned to our rooms to prepare our gear and try to get some sleep. Again, it did not come easily.

6

BEST IF USED BY DATE

The world breaks everyone
and afterward many are strong in the broken places.
But those that will not break it kills.

ERNEST HEMINGWAY

Not long after being diagnosed with Parkinson's disease, my career stalled. Although I was able to continue working, the possibility of quick advancement in a new subsidiary company and new facility that many of my coworkers still enjoyed slipped from my grasp. The Parkinson's medications seemed to be working most of the time, but Dr. Nicholas and I were always trying to find the right cocktail to control the symptoms that plagued me while also reducing the side effects of the medications.

My legs did not return to normal, as if the mere distance from my brain prevented them from functioning properly. Rigid and able to move only in short, shuffle steps, they felt nearly useless. They were the most noticeable and constant reminder of my brain's failing ability to control my body. Less outwardly noticeable was the crushing fatigue and chronic sleepiness that accompany Parkinson's and Parkinson's medications.

Although I didn't like it, I understood the reluctance of those in positions of power to see me as someone with a promising future. Even I wondered how long I would be able to do the job I was being paid to do, much less be able to take on and excel at additional tasks and responsibilities. Unsaid, the words seemed to follow me everywhere. *Progressive. Degenerative. No cure.* Many times, my subconscious mind added the word, *Prison.*

Instead of the promise of possible future advancement in a great organization that had led us to make the move to Alabama, my focus shifted to trying to hang on for as long as possible. I had to work harder each day just to maintain my capabilities and to fulfill my responsibilities. I felt like I had an expiration date, similar to the ones on milk cartons, printed on my forehead: Best if used by (date).

While my career was in jeopardy, my relationship with family wasn't. Parkinson's helped me to understand that my family was much more important than my career. There had been times when I allowed my ambition to dominate my thoughts, but with each day my battle with Parkinson's taught me what was really important.

My career had been a measuring stick of success in the world and my way of providing for my wife and sons—to give them things I didn't have growing up. Because of the battle with Parkinson's, I grew to understand that life isn't about a career or the acquisition of things.

Liv and I had been through thick and thin, so I rarely had concerns about her resolve when the "in sickness" time came. She had seen her grandmother suffer from Alzheimer's for years and had helped care for her mother as she fought a relatively short battle with ALS before her death barely into her sixties. Now her husband was fighting a battle with Parkinson's.

It was in times like these when she shined brilliantly. Her strong, resilient nature and her love and caring were so much more than I deserved. She never made me feel like less of a man because my legs didn't work like they should or because I couldn't control what my body was or was not doing. In my darkest moments, I wondered if I should have the kindness to end the battle myself and release her to live a normal life.

The boys accepted that I had taken a hit, but I was still the same dad. I wanted to use the Parkinson's—or more precisely how I lived with it—as a daily teaching tool for them. Kids are so resilient. If mom and dad are okay with whatever obstacle comes their way, kids usually accept things and move on. In retrospect, I believe it also taught them about having compassion and empathy for others.

Our sons have been vastly different from the day Max was born. Liv has said many times that Eli has my heart and Max has my mind. Much to their good fortune, both received their mother's loving, caring spirit. At first glance, it's not easy to tell they are brothers. Eli has my coloring. He is dark-eyed and dark-haired with a slight olive tint of skin. Max has the fair skin, blond hair, and blue eyes of Liv's English-Irish heritage. As adults, Max is the tallest of our family.

Both are fiercely independent, but show it in different ways. Eli always seemed like the hero in a Greek tragedy, a physically and mentally tough dreamer destined to do great things, but with a foreboding sense of loss or suffering. He is a loving person, extremely loyal to his family and friends. He's willing to take great risks for a person he cares about or a cause he believes in. He's the kind of person who draws to him people from all walks of life. Instinctual almost to a fault, he trusts his heart to lead him in the direction he must go.

Max, on the other hand, has an inner calmness that radiates to those around him, assuring them that he will always be okay. We rarely worry about him. He's magical around small children, yet most comfortable with people much older than himself. He's perfectly content in his own company with keen analytical skills and a desire to seek knowledge about many things. When I struggled with the effects of Parkinson's, he would often place his hand on my shoulder, touch his forehead to mine, and with a purposefully goofy grin and a childlike innocence, he would assure me that things would get better.

As great as my family life was, like many people with Young Onset Parkinson's disease, I still had a mortgage, car payment, and a long list of other financial obligations. I often wondered how long we would be able to maintain this way of life. At times, I felt like Atlas holding the weight of the world on my shoulders. What I didn't know then is that stress greatly exacerbates the symptoms. I had Parkinson's, which made my ordinary life difficult ... which made working difficult ... which caused stress ... which caused the effects of Parkinson's to worsen. The perpetual motion of this cycle became a downward spiral that I couldn't control. I was able to hold it together reasonably well for the first few years after diagnosis, or so I thought at the time, but the clock was counting down to the end of the life I had built. It became so loud at times I thought it would drive me insane. The clock stopped ticking almost four years to the day after our initial visit with Dr. Nicholas.

7

KILIMANJARO:
DAY 1 - MACHAME GATE

24 AUG 2012

The day started earlier than I wanted when I finally surrendered to consciousness after a second night of anxious, restless sleep since arriving in country. I crept from my bed to the shower a full hour and a half before my alarm was set to go off as to not wake Dan or Brad sooner than necessary, especially since it would be the last time any of us would see a mattress for most of the next week. I arrived at the breakfast dining area a few minutes later to find that I wasn't the only one who was up early. Several of my teammates were already there, eating generous portions of the bland breakfast bar items. None of us knew when we would next eat, so we stocked up while we had the chance.

With our water resistant duffel bags in a large pile and backpacks by our sides, we mingled in the lobby of the hotel waiting on the ride that would take us from Arusha to the base of Kilimanjaro to begin our journey. Most of the group had visited the currency exchange inside the hotel the previous day to swap dollars for shillings to tip the guides, porters and cooks at the end of our trek, but a few were making last-minute exchanges. Excitement and anxiety hovered in the air around us.

When the same bus that had brought us to the hotel from the airport finally arrived, we helped our driver load the bags and took photos posing and pointing at the holographic image of Jesus displayed in the front windshield before packing ourselves into the cramped bus. I hoped our bags, piled high on top of the bus and strapped down with rope, would survive the trip to the Machame Gate. Several cartons of eggs and other fresh foods that would be part of our meals for the next six days were loaded last, obstructing the aisle of the bus. Excited conversations and laughter filled the bus during the hour and a half ride through several small villages before arriving at the Machame Gate.

At 5,942 feet above sea level, the Machame Gate was the starting point of our trek (Stedman, 2010, p. 264). The gate itself was simple, made of iron and covered by a thin metal A-frame structure. Outside the gate some locals waited and beckoned, hoping for work as a last-minute replacement or extra porter. Others attempted to sell trinkets to the trekkers. Just inside the gate, a small A-frame building housed an office where every group must register. Behind the A-frame were restrooms where anyone over 5'5" should duck before entering.

Another larger building sat up a slight hill next to the parking lot where buses stopped and quickly unloaded. Blue monkeys roamed the corrugated metal roof of the large building watching the festivities, hoping for a scrap of food from a generous benefactor. Between the A-frame office and the larger building was a covered area filled with picnic tables, and a few more blue monkeys hoping for a free meal. This is where I waited, practicing the patience that would be required over the next several days. As I settled in for the wait, I began to understand one undeniably important reality of Kilimanjaro. The mountain operates on its own time and will not be rushed.

After writing my info in the registration book, I found a perch on the waist-high outer wall of the covered picnic area where I could watch all that was going on around me. I surveyed the activity in the parking lot above us where the porters were weighing duffel bags and divvying up other items to be carried up the mountain. There were several groups at different spots going through the various phases of registration, final preparation, and staging while awaiting approval to start their trek up the Machame Route.

Known as the Whiskey Route, the trail is now the most popular of the six climbing routes on Kilimanjaro, and the most scenic. Most popular does not mean it's the easiest, but it does accommodate an additional day or two for acclimatization if needed. It's known as the Whiskey Route (as in "the hard stuff") in contrast to the previously most popular and easier route, Marangu (Stedman, 2010, p. 263). The Marangu Route is known as the Coca-Cola trail or "Tourist Route" in reference to the large number of climbers who sleep in campsite huts along the route, which is considered a luxury on the mountain (Stedman, 2010, p. 241). We would not be sleeping in huts on the Machame Route.

I observed everyone around me, making odds on their chances of success to pass the time. A large group of Brits looked young and physically fit enough, but I doubted that any of them had a realistic idea of what lay ahead of them or the risks they were about to take. Another large group waited at the A-frame completing the registration process. Composed mostly of American teens, the group was led by a smaller group of adults who appeared to be seasoned hikers. A small group of cocky European men in their twenties waited impatiently on the other side of the covered picnic area.

Our group appeared to be the most prepared, but, I admit, that is only because I understood our reasons for coming to the mountain. Most of us were more than a decade older than the large group of British climbers and the group of American high school kids, and at least a few years older than nearly everyone else beginning the climb that morning. At forty-six, I had the distinction of being the oldest member of our group. I was also the most motivated. It wasn't just a function of age. We were more seasoned by the successes and failures of life. This wasn't an ordinary vacation trip for most of us.

Sixteen members made up our group, but within the group was a team of ten. Our journey began seven months earlier. Living in different parts of the United States, we communicated via social media and by phone, discussing everything from gear to clothing to how to pack for the trip, but most importantly why we had decided to take on this challenge. We wanted to enjoy the journey, but reaching the goal was far more important. We had a singular purpose, and we were focused. We were also deeply invested because we were doing this for others we cared about: To do our part to help end their suffering.

In *Lucky Man*, Michael J. Fox wrote, "If you were to rush into this room right now and announce that you had struck a deal—with God, Allah, Buddha, Christ, Krishna, Bill Gates, whomever—in which the ten years since my diagnosis could be magically taken away, traded in for ten more years as the person I was before—I would, without a moment's hesitation, tell you to take a hike" (Fox, 2002, pp. 5-6).

I remember reading the quote in the first year after my diagnosis and found it to be awe-inspiring. More than that, I thought it was incredible that he could have suffered like he had, yet have such a positive outlook on life. As I look back on how I felt after first being told that I have Parkinson's—anxious about the unknown and the struggle ahead of me—I didn't know if I could ever have the same perspective, but I hoped I would.

I didn't want Parkinson's disease. Yet, I had longed to be like Fox in one regard. I wanted to be a better man ten years in the future in spite of Parkinson's, or perhaps, because of it. Waiting here, almost ten years after my own diagnosis and just steps away from beginning the most important walk of my life, I could speak his words with the same conviction, as if they were my own.

Elements of his statement were also prophetic in a way for my own life. I was here to climb Mt. Kilimanjaro because Michael J. Fox had, in essence, provided an extraordinary opportunity to "take a hike" to the summit of the tallest free-standing mountain on Earth. I had lived through my own personal hell and had become a totally different person because of it. Making it to the top of this mountain would prove I had escaped from what I had believed for years was an inescapable prison. More importantly, it could show others in the midst of their battles that which is possible in their lives.

8

A TANGIBLE ENCOUNTER

*Out of suffering have emerged the strongest souls;
the most massive characters are seared with scars.*

KAHLIL GIBRAN

I f one accepts the premise of the five stages of grief, made famous by Elisabeth Kübler-Ross in her book, *On Death and Dying*, as a valid model for how we accept loss in our lives, then it took years for me to progress through most of them. It's not about the life-changing illness that is Parkinson's, but rather the imminent death of the life that I had worked so hard to build.

Of the proposed five stages of grief—denial, anger, bargaining, depression, and acceptance—I believe I skipped over the anger phase for the most part (Kübler-Ross, 1969). Aside from the initial anger with the first few doctors I saw before my diagnosis, and being frustrated/angry at times, I don't recall being angry about my circumstances as an ongoing stage or phase. I attribute the lack of anger to my simple faith that

God knows what's going on and that He has a reason for everything that happens. Although difficult at times, I do trust Him.

I believe the denial and bargaining phases were combined in my case, and think of that period of time as the "hanging on years." Considering what we were facing, I believe we did a good job of hanging on. Although counter to everything I had been taught, letting go would have been the better course of action. For me, hanging on consisted of clinging to normalcy by denying how quickly Parkinson's was progressing, while hoping and believing that I could continue to work until the boys were out of school. Fear of what would happen when I could no longer hang on hovered in the back of my mind. The sense of being hunted was so vivid I could almost feel it like a tingle on my skin.

Depression moved through my life at glacial speed. Its progression was difficult to see, yet it moved with incredible force as it slowly carved away at my spirit. Acceptance was so distant, seemingly unreachable. The confluence of life events and the toll that Parkinson's had taken on my body would come together sooner than I had hoped, to end the life I had worked so hard to build. I felt hopeless, unable to stop it from happening.

In the summer of 2006, Dr. Nicholas and I agreed that I should take a leave of absence from work to focus on adjusting the medication cocktail because it just wasn't working for me. I was missing more and more days at work and it was becoming an issue. If my career was to be prolonged, I needed a reset. Adjusting the dosages of the different medications can cause periods of nausea, extreme sleepiness (somnolence), or sleeping for unusually long periods of time (hypersomnia).

It would be extremely difficult to maintain a consistent work schedule while making the changes in medications.

In addition to the physical issues I faced, Liv and I were dealing with Eli. He wasn't in or causing trouble. He was simply approaching adulthood at an ever-increasing pace. During the summer before his senior year of high school, he reaffirmed his intention to join the Marine Corps as soon as he graduated. He wanted to enter the Delayed Entry Program (DEP) to begin preparation and to assure that he would get the job classification he desired more than any other: Infantry Marine. Later in the process, a Marine recruiter told us that hardly anyone "DEPed in" to ensure a spot in the Infantry, because the majority of those enlisting in the Marine Corps would most likely be assigned to an Infantry battalion anyway. Eli knew this, but wanted to ensure that he would have the opportunity for combat. Liv and I weren't facing the typical feelings of letting go of our oldest child like a lot of parents do. We were facing letting go of our son so he could go to war.

We finally let go of Eli during the summer of 2006. We stopped questioning his decision to become a Marine, and allowed him to take ownership of his decision. We realized that we, as parents, did not control his destiny. Although cautious at first, he seized upon our sincerity and began his life journey. It would shape not only his life, but all of our lives in a major way.

I'm not sure that a clear line between depression and acceptance exists. It's more like an overlapping, concurrent progression as the former slowly becomes the latter. One morning during my leave of absence from work, I went to my workshop in the basement and sat on a stool next to my worktable for the next three days. I'm not sure if it was the Parkinson's, the weight of the stress, a good old-fashioned anxiety attack, or a combination thereof, but I sat there frozen, thinking.

I must have taken bathroom breaks, eaten a meal or two, and taken my meds, but I don't recall doing so. Some people may call what I went through over those three days a mental breakdown, but I don't think it was. It was a time of honesty, an evaluation of my life path: where I had been, where I had always thought I was going, where I currently was, and an increasingly bleak future.

There were times over the years when I wondered if I could bear to live another day. I had grown to hate my body for what it had done to my life. But, if I gave up, what message would it send to my family? I had invested so much of myself in my family. I just had to know how the stories of their lives would progress. No matter how much I suffered, the tether that enabled me to live another day, then another, was my family.

As I tried to focus on specific events or relationships, my mind kept steering me toward another time and place from my childhood. It was my first tangible encounter with God.

The gravel bit into his skin as he dropped to his knees and cried out, "Please strike me dead. I can't take it anymore!" He slumped forward, defeated, and the tears rolled down his prepubescent face and mixed with the sweat. The July heat and the mosquitos didn't bother him. Despair was his constant companion.

He wasn't sure why he had chosen this place for what he hoped would be his end. The gravel road at the end of his street had no traffic. Coming to an abrupt halt at the base of a hill roughly a quarter-mile from the chained boundary where the pavement ended, it had been cut into the overgrown East Tennessee pasture several years earlier by a developer who went bankrupt before the first house had been built. The boy didn't know these details or who owned the land and the old gravel road, nor did he care. It was the first place he thought of to go as he left his house, still feeling the sting on the left side of his face.

He was still unsure if he really believed in God or Jesus, but he had seen his mother kneel in prayer in her darkest hours. The fact that he was kneeling surprised him, but he didn't know what else to do. He didn't want to hurt anymore. He didn't want his mom to hurt anymore. She did her best to protect him whenever his father's drunken, sarcastic, and mean-spirited words ran dry and he would resort to violence. He begged God again and again to end his life. The tears flowed as he awaited God's decision, certain that if a loving God existed, He would end his suffering.

When he woke, the first thing he saw was the beautiful blue sky. As he lay on his back and focused on the perfect clouds, he realized that he had cried himself to sleep. He didn't remember making his way into the tall grass of the pasture. The despair that had consumed him for so long was gone, and what took its place was something he had rarely known, especially for someone so young: peace and hope. God had answered his prayers, but in a totally unexpected way. The bolt of lightning he had begged for had not descended from the heavens to end his life. Instinctively, he knew he had been spared for a reason, but he had no idea why.

As he stood, he raised his arms toward the sky, partly mimicking a runner who had just finished a race, but mostly as a child's way of saying thanks—it was a gesture he would repeat many times throughout his life yet lived. Everything he had been through up until that moment no longer mattered. He was still living and breathing, thus, he believed his life must have a purpose. Finding and fulfilling that purpose became the fuel that propelled him forward.

Why did this seldom thought of memory dominate my thoughts during those three days? I needed to think about so many other things, but I kept coming back to this specific memory. I believe it was God's gentle way of helping me to see some truths.

I had been here before. I had been to the breaking point, that place where I'm out of options, and I feel defeated. I had been to a similar place in life before and had not only come through it, but I had thrived afterward.

I am not in control. God is. Had I ever been in control? For the first time in my adult life, I realized that God rules everything. The good and the bad things in life happen for a reason. I was able to see all the good things that had happened in my life since that day in the pasture when I was just a little boy with a broken spirit. It gave me a new perspective.

There is hope. Where there is hope, there is peace. I was alive, so I must have a purpose not yet fulfilled. How could this disease, this monster, this prison, be used for something positive?

When I went down to my basement workshop, the weight of my world was crushing me. When I came up from the basement, I was less burdened. The issues facing our family were just as real as they were prior, but I saw them in a different light. Liv and the boys could tell something had changed for the better. They didn't question it. They just rolled with it, which was something they were much better at doing than I had been.

9

KILIMANJARO:
DAY 1 - THE CLIMB BEGINS

24 AUG 2012

The paperwork was complete, and the porters and others supporting our group had gone on ahead of us on their way to the first camp, located near where the rainforest transitions from land dense with tall trees and vegetation to the heath zone, where rolling hills are populated with much smaller, shrub-like heather plants.

Several minutes after the British group was given approval to begin trekking, we were given the green light to proceed. Suited up in our hiking gear and light-weight rain/wind jackets with our backpacks strapped to our bodies and trekking poles adjusted to the perfect height, we posed for a group photo in front of the Machame Gate before beginning the climb. There were sixteen members of our group.

Will serves multiple roles. He's an athletic man in his mid-twenties with the life experience of someone much older. He is the American representative of the adventure travel company responsible for our climb, a Team Fox member, and an employee of the Michael J. Fox Foundation for Parkinson's Research (MJFF). He spends many of his days off leading hikes for the adventure travel company, mostly in the areas surrounding New York City. We refer to him as "our fearless leader."

Grace serves as the Associate Director of Team Fox for MJFF. She's 30-ish, a runner, a CrossFit junkie, and so much more. Bright and outgoing, she became involved with Team Fox before going to work for MJFF. Her father has been fighting Parkinson's for more than a decade.

Noah is Grace's older brother. A Team Fox member in his early thirties, he might be the funniest person in the group. He's the art director for a snowboard manufacturer and an amateur chef. Like his sister, his participation in the climb is for his father.

Dan is the second oldest of the group at 41. He's a Team Fox member and mentor. A marathon runner and a professional employee of the University of Michigan, he and his family live in Ann Arbor. He's raised thousands of dollars for Team Fox in the past few years and is climbing Kilimanjaro in memory of his late father who fought the good fight against Parkinson's.

Brad is the youngest member of the "old man club" and a Team Fox member in his late thirties. A tall, avid outdoorsman originally from Iowa, he and his young family live on the outskirts of New York City. His dry sense of humor and attention to detail are exemplary. He is the tech wizard of the group and has both a family connection and work connection to Parkinson's.

Annie and *Drew* are Team Fox members in their early thirties. Annie is a marathon runner, hiker, and a senior director for an educational testing company. Drew is a hiker, runner, and an attorney in Manhattan. He's in a close race with Noah for the funniest person in the group. The engaged couple's rapport with each other is hilarious. Originally, Drew supported Annie in her involvement with Team Fox because her dad is battling Parkinson's then, few years later, Drew's father was diagnosed with Parkinson's.

Helen and *Nick,* also in their early thirties, are Team Fox members from the Atlanta area. She's an attorney and he's a business executive. Athletes with a love for the outdoors, they were both celebrating their first wedding anniversary and climbing Kilimanjaro to support a family friend with Parkinson's. We connected quickly, as they are the only other native Southerners in our group.

The remaining six members of our group did not come to Africa to raise funds for Parkinson's research. Although their personal motivations for making the climb were different from the Team Fox members of our group, we meshed as teammates from the moment we met.

Ava is thirty. A bright, athletic, and wickedly funny physical therapist, she lives in upstate New York. From other members of the group to the guides, porters, and other Tanzanian support personnel, everyone walked away from the briefest encounter with her a happier person.

Lizzie is thirty, and Ava's best friend and college roommate. She's a kind young woman with a classical beauty and an infectious smile. In addition to her career in the financial district in New York City, she's a dancer and an experienced hiker.

Kate, in her early thirties, is a nurse at a prominent cancer treatment center in New York City. Quiet and a bit shy, she's the mother of a young son. The Kilimanjaro climb is an unexpected adventure. She came at the urging of her friend and coworker, Bella.

Bella is small bundle of energy in her late twenties. She's in her element outdoors, and always has a smile on her face. Also a nurse at the cancer treatment center in New York City where Kate works, she's an experienced hiker and adventure seeker. A few months earlier, she had traveled to Peru where she hiked the Inca Trail to Machu Picchu to explore the fifteenth century mountain top site, the most famous representation of Inca civilization. She has dreamed of climbing Mt. Kilimanjaro for quite some time.

Alex is an energetic holistic health and wellness coach in her mid twenties who runs her own business in New York City. She's climbing Kilimanjaro to raise awareness and funds for traumatic brain injury research. Her love for her brother, a traumatic brain injury survivor, has led her to climb the mountain.

Tyler, a nurse in his mid twenties, works at a hospital in northern New Jersey. He's a tall, handsome young man. An experienced outdoorsman, he is excited about and extremely interested in people and what makes them tick. He is close to the same age as my sons, and he reminds me of them. He and I are paired as hiking partners for the climb.

I'm the oldest member of the group, but not an old man. I'm a Team Fox member and the only person in the group who has Parkinson's disease. Climbing Kilimanjaro has been my sole focus for several months, and I've made some drastic life changes in order to be here. My teammates understand just how important this climb is to me.

My involvement with the Michael J. Fox Foundation and Team Fox, the grassroots, community fundraising arm of MJFF, was my first tangible foray into Parkinson's advocacy. Like my Parkinson's mentor, I lived with the disease for years before emerging from the isolation to take on an active role in being part of the solution.

On September 28, 1999, in testimony before the Senate Appropriations Subcommittee on Labor, Health and Human Services, and Education, Michael J. Fox stated, "What I understood very clearly is that the time for 'quietly soldiering on' is through. The war against Parkinson's is a winnable war and I have resolved to play a role in that victory" (Government Printing Office, 1999, p. 12).

In 2000, Fox teamed with Debi Brooks, a former vice president at Goldman Sachs, to create the Michael J. Fox Foundation for Parkinson's Research (The Michael J. Fox, 2012, "Foxfeed Blog: Debi Brooks"). In his book, *Lucky Man*, Fox states as his vision for the Foundation, "Our goal as an institution was nothing less than planned obsolescence. What I had in mind was an organization built for speed, eschewing bureaucracy and taking an entrepreneurial approach toward helping researchers do what they say can be done: find a cure for Parkinson's within a decade" (Fox, 2002, pp. 248-249).

Since inception, the Michael J. Fox Foundation for Parkinson's Research has become the largest private funder of Parkinson's disease research in the world, investing hundreds of millions of dollars in research. As of May 2015, eighty-nine cents of every dollar donated to the Foundation was directed to research programs (The Michael J. Fox, 2015, "Financials"). According to the prominent charitable organization review sites, Charity Navigator and Charity Watch, the Foundation has earned their highest ratings (Charity Navigator, 2015; Charity Watch, 2015).

In addition to the funding of innovative research to find the cure, the Foundation has had an unprecedented influence upon involving the Parkinson's community, both people living with Parkinson's and their caregivers. In the effort to find the cure, patients are actively recruited for participation in clinical studies, and provided with connections to clinical trials, opportunities, and support for involvement in fundraising activities (The Michael J. Fox, 2015, "Participate").

In response to the overwhelming desire of the Parkinson's community to be involved in fundraising for the Foundation, Team Fox was created in 2006. Since its creation, Team Fox members have raised millions of dollars for Parkinson's research. Each year, hundreds of people are actively involved in creating and carrying out various fundraising activities including participation in marathons and other running events, hiking mountains around the world, bicycle rides and races, pancake breakfasts, concerts, candy sales, dinner events, young professionals groups in major cities, and many other projects (The Michael J. Fox, 2015, "Get Involved"). Over the years, a few Team Fox members have chosen to climb Mt. Kilimanjaro on their own to raise funds for the Foundation, but our team's climb is the first to be initiated by the Foundation.

Standing beneath the Machame Gate, we were excited and ready to begin the climb. Steven, our lead Tanzanian guide, snapped many photos of our group with several of our cameras. Although he speaks English extremely well, Steven took a moment to teach us a few Swahili words that we would hear and use often.

He asked the question I had waited months to hear. "Are we ready to go?" Then, in Swahili: "*Twende?*"

He then taught us how to reply affirmatively in Swahili. We repeated the enthusiastic reply in unison, "*Sawa sawa!*"

With the question asked and answered, we began the five-day ascent to the summit of Mt. Kilimanjaro.

10

THE DECONSTRUCTION OF A MAN

It's not whether you get knocked down,
it's whether you get up.

Vince Lombardi

Six years before beginning the Kilimanjaro climb, I began a new phase of my life. As I walked out of the auto plant for the last time, I questioned if I was ready for what life had in store for me next. *Am I ready to go?* The day I had been dreading for four years had arrived, yet I was still alive and my world had not ended. I was forty years old and my career was over.

During my medical leave from work, I got some much needed rest, and the reset of my medication cocktail seemed to have the needed effect upon managing the Parkinson's. I returned to work in the fall of 2006 with the renewed hope I could continue my career for an extended period of time, but it wasn't meant to be. Once I returned to work, the demands and the stress quickly took their toll and my body did not respond well. Finally, I approached Jake to discuss my situation and get his opinion regarding my ability to continue working. We sat in a break area on the production floor, the massive machinery that produces a new vehicle once every couple of minutes surrounding us.

Jake lit a cigarette, looked me straight in the eyes and said, "You know I love you like a brother, right?"

"Yeah, I know." I replied.

"I know you're all about leaving everything on the field," he said, referring to my days as a high school football player. "But you need to look around. Everyone who was in the stands has gone home, and the lights are being turned off. You understand what I'm saying?"

"Just say it, Jake," I said, suddenly aware of where the conversation was heading.

He took a long draw on the cigarette, exhaled slowly, and said, "I think it is time, but you're the only one who can make that decision."

With those words, I knew my career was coming to an end. It wasn't a surprise. We talked about it for more than an hour after he spoke the words that I had dreaded hearing for years. Jake had struggled with it for a long time as well. He was my close friend, but he also had to balance his responsibilities for achieving production goals and managing more than a thousand workers.

In his matter-of-fact way, Jake said, "Look, it's not like you smoked a pack of cigs a day since you were a kid and got sick because of something you did, or did something stupid to get fired. You didn't get in the serving line and ask for a generous portion of Parkinson's disease. Stuff happens and you just have to deal with it the best way you can."

I trusted him. Although he has a gruff exterior at work, Jake is a caring, loyal man. One thing he said really struck a chord with me. "As your friend, I want you to go and enjoy the time you have left. I want you to go do the things you want to do before you can no longer do them." Neither of us knew at that time what those things were, or where they would take me.

I think of those next few years as "the deconstruction of a man." It was as if God placed me on His work bench and began the work of tearing apart everything I had been. The process was initiated long before the first signs of Parkinson's, when the cells in my brain that make dopamine began dying.

God began stripping away all that I had worked to achieve, with the exception of my family. With my health in rapid decline, He had taken my career and cast it aside. Along with my career, He dismantled my status and title. Men are built in this way: We gain pride and a self-identity from our jobs. Ask most men who they are and they might tell you they are a husband and/or a father, but most likely will spend the most time and words reciting their job title and telling you what they do for a living. What we do is part of our identity, and I was no different.

With the loss of my career came the loss of most of my income. With the loss of income, it meant the loss of material possessions would soon follow. The first thing to go was the dream house. Liv and I were heartbroken the day the For Sale sign was placed in the front yard, but we knew we had no other viable alternative. Our castle would soon be gone. The new automobiles and extra furniture went next. Essentially, we began selling everything we did not need.

We struggled financially during the several months between leaving work and the sale of the house. We hated that the upheaval and uncertainty was happening during the last six months of Eli's time living at home with us. The house was sold, ironically, to another employee of the company I had just left who was beginning his career with them. The minivans and SUVs made at the plant would continue to indirectly pay the mortgage payments on the house.

The frame of the painting that represented our lives was now gone, and the edges of the canvas were tattered. The colors that surrounded the characters in the painting were fading, yet the colors that shaped the characters remained vibrant. A few months before the house sold, Eli left home to begin his life in the Marine Corps. An empty seat at the table was now part of the battered painting. With some much needed good fortune, we found another house in the same neighborhood. It was much simpler and much smaller than our dream house, but it was home.

11

SOLITARY CONFINEMENT

*Yet a part of you still believes you can fight and
survive no matter what your mind knows. It's not
so strange. Where there's still life, there's still hope.
What happens is up to God.*

LOUIS ZAMPERINI

Eli's unit deployed to Ramadi, Al Anbar Province, Iraq,
during the fall of 2008. Al Anbar Province in western Iraq is the only Sunni dominated province in
the country. A major counterinsurgency campaign had been
waged by the United States military and the Iraqi government
from 2004 until 2008, although most of the heavy fighting
had ended in 2007.

We heard from Eli periodically during the seven-month
deployment, and each time he reported that he was doing
well and hadn't seen much action. We never knew if he was
telling the truth, or telling white lies to keep us from worrying

about him. It was our family's indoctrination into the world of those left behind.

We reluctantly went on with our lives, but a part of us was always on the other side of the world with Eli. The yellow ribbon and bow around the tree in our front yard reminded us and our neighbors that we were awaiting the return of a loved one serving in a war zone. If anyone had asked, I could have told them how many days remained until his anticipated homecoming.

I did have a wonderful distraction, though. Max was coming into his own. After fourteen years of being little brother, he relished stepping out of Eli's shadow. Eli had our sole attention for the first four of our parenting years before Max was born. Max would have our sole attention at home on a daily basis during the last four years living with us. I didn't just love Max like crazy, I needed him, too. He was my right hand. During the first two years of my forced retirement, my health worsened significantly. I had hoped the removal of work stress would slow the progression of the disease, but it seemed the opposite was true.

Between the onset of Parkinson's in 2002 and late 2008, I gained eighty pounds (eventually ballooning to more than three-hundred pounds). The combination of fighting Parkinson's, the side effects of the Parkinson's medications, and lack of exercise was becoming a lethal combination. Much information has come to light over the past few years regarding the possible side effects of dopamine receptor agonists. Agonists are the primary category of medications used to treat Parkinson's other than the gold standard, Sinemet (carbidopa/levodopa). The levodopa component of Sinemet is converted into dopamine by the body. A dopamine agonist acts like dopamine by stimulating the nerve receptors that would normally be stimulated by dopamine.

One such side effect of dopamine agonists is compulsive behavior. For some Parkinson's patients, the compulsive behavior can include poor impulse control. For others like me, it can lead to devastating effects from compulsive gambling, shopping, eating, uncontrollable sexual urges/activity, or other compulsive behaviors. Fortunately, I was never prone to the more severe compulsive behaviors. Instead, I spent time in large home improvement stores shopping for bigger, better power tools, and eating several times a day trying to satisfy an insatiable hunger. At least the tools were useful. I was always hungry, and just assumed the meds drove the hunger from a physiological standpoint. I now believe differently. (Moore, Glenmullen & Mattison, 2014).

One Parkinson's medication I used also caused a particularly debilitating side effect: narcolepsy, or falling asleep without notice. Sometimes this occurred mid-sentence, other times it would occur while performing tasks like driving. I felt like an elderly person who becomes a danger when driving, at risk of losing his driver's license and his freedom. Max went most places with me to keep me from falling asleep. More than once, he was scared out of his mind when I unexpectedly fell asleep at the wheel. I seriously considered giving up driving, but held on tightly and selfishly to one of the last parts of my independence.

An additional medication was added to the cocktail, one to treat narcolepsy, a side effect of a drug prescribed to treat the symptoms of Parkinson's disease. The medications and side effects were like complex pieces of a puzzle, and I often wondered if going unmedicated and just dealing with the symptoms of the Parkinson's disease would be better.

Like many Americans who become morbidly overweight, I developed other health problems, known as co-morbidities.

My primary care physician cautioned me about the weight gain every time I saw her, and I heard the same from Dr. Nicholas at our regular appointments. I developed sleep apnea, and was told by a doctor specializing in sleep disorders to use a CPAP machine when I slept or risk dying. I developed Type II diabetes, and was at risk of blindness, amputation of limbs, or other horrible complications. I couldn't believe this had happened to me. I had been healthy, strong, and fit for most of my adult life up until I got the Parkinson's diagnosis.

Parkinson's is typically one-sided, meaning that the limbs on one side of the body will be considerably more affected by tremors and/or muscle rigidity. My left side is much worse than my right side. For that I'm somewhat grateful because I'm right-handed. As the Parkinson's progressed, I developed dystonia (the contraction and twisting of muscles), which is often associated with Parkinson's (The Michael J. Fox, 2015, "Dystonia"). The primary targets were my left leg and arm. My leg twisted inward, my left foot almost perpendicular to my right foot at times, and walking became not only more difficult but extremely painful as well.

Dr. Nicholas gave me options, and I chose the mechanical option because I didn't want one more foreign substance entering my body. I went to the prosthetics lab at UAB where a prosthetist constructed a lightweight leg brace hinged at the ankle to help keep my leg straight. Combined with a cane I was still able to walk, though it was laborious and odd looking.

In my early forties, I had Parkinson's disease, was significantly overweight with an undiagnosed, compulsive eating disorder and narcolepsy (side effects of medications), sleep apnea and Type II diabetes (caused by the weight gain), used a cane and a leg brace to walk, and took multiple medications.

I was the recipient of warnings from multiple physicians that I needed to do something or my condition would worsen, perhaps leading to death. Maintaining a positive outlook was becoming more difficult by the day, and that was just dealing with the physical issues.

The psychological issues followed a similar trajectory. I had a son fighting in a war in Iraq. Worrying about him drained my remaining energy. After being forced to retire, I spent much of my time isolated, with Max at school and Liv at work. I avoided mirrors and shied away from being photographed. I couldn't stand to see the person I had become on the outside. When I wasn't sleeping, I kept busy working on projects in my garage workshop a few hours per day, but missed the camaraderie of working with my friends.

Many people long for a time when they can leave work and do whatever they feel like doing on any given day. In my case, it was as if I had been told to go sit on the bench and watch the other kids play ball. I reluctantly accepted my lot in life and tried to make the best of it, but it became increasingly difficult. I wasn't sure I had much fight left in me, and questioned God often during those lonely days, asking what purpose He had for my suffering and isolation.

The isolation became more prevalent as the days and months wore on. I became more withdrawn from society in large part. I wanted people to see me as the person I used to be, not a walking billboard for disease or affliction. I felt as though I couldn't even enter a convenience store to buy a drink or pay for gas without drawing unwanted looks or questions. I grew frustrated with the sheer ignorance and lack of tact in other people's interactions with me. I could have been having a good day physically and emotionally, which was rare, and a straight up stupid question from a total stranger would both anger me and crush my spirit. More than once, I was asked, "What's wrong with your legs?" or "Why do you walk with a cane?" What's wrong with a simple, "Hey," or "How are you?"

I even withdrew from church. The one place I expected to get some peace and comfort in my struggle became just another spoke in the broken wheel. I had hoped to be able to go about my personal business of worshipping a God and Savior that I still believed in with all my heart, despite the difficulties and challenges that Parkinson's had caused in the lives of my family, but it just didn't happen. I wanted to blend in with like-minded people and focus on something greater than my physical being, but the unwanted attention never ceased. Someone always wanted to make a big deal about adding the crippled man to a prayer list, but no one ever offered to help in any applicable way. I was alone on this path. I didn't forsake my belief in God, but I didn't want anyone else's participation in my relationship with Him. My isolation from the world outside of my family and a few close friends was complete.

Our lives changed for the better with the reduced stress of Eli returning home from a war zone, but we understood that the respite would be brief. By the time Eli went to Iraq, the war there was beginning to wind down. Although the Iraq deployment was hard for us as a family left at home waiting for him to return, at least we knew the war in Iraq was approaching an end. The deployment was relatively uneventful, and 2d Battalion, 9th Marines, returned to the United States with no Marines killed in action.

Life moved forward, regardless of illness, or war, or other obstacles. For a brief moment, we were a complete family again. It gave me hope that I could hang on to life for a while longer, that there were still reasons to live and not succumb to accepting that my life could soon come to an end. As the war in Iraq moved toward conclusion, the war in Afghanistan was heating up. It loomed on the horizon as did my failing health, somehow destined to converge.

12

ECHO TO MARJAH (HELL, PART 1)

If ever there is a tomorrow when we're not together...
there is something you must always remember.
You are braver than you believe,
stronger than you seem,
and smarter than you think.
But the most important thing is,
even if we're apart ...
I'll always be with you.

(CHRISTOPHER ROBIN TO WINNIE-THE-POOH)
A.A. MILNE

Afghanistan deployment day began like many other days in my life. Take my meds, drink a large mug of coffee while waiting for the meds to kick in, shower, dress, and eat breakfast. But it wasn't like most other days. My son would leave for a dangerous destination thousands of miles away from us, and I didn't know if he would be coming home. There was no way of comprehending it at the time, but new life—*my new life*—was conceived that day.

In December of 2009, the President announced the impending deployment of 30,000 additional troops to Afghanistan in the spring and early summer of 2010. Nearly 8,000 Marines from Camp Lejeune, NC, were to be part of the troop surge, Eli's unit among them. The 2/9 was to deploy to the Marjah district in Helmand Province in southern Afghanistan, an area rife with poppy fields, a major source of funding for the Taliban.

Two weeks before deployment day, Eli made it home for pre-deployment leave just in time for the Independence Day holiday weekend. We hosted a large gathering of family, friends, and neighbors so Eli could see everyone before he left the country. It appeared to be a normal backyard summer party with a cookout, people talking, laughing, and sharing stories, and kids running around playing games with rules only they understood.

Although Eli seemed to enjoy being with everyone, I could see the faraway look in his eyes from time to time. It was one that only a parent can understand from studying and loving his or her child since birth. He was with us, but a part of his soul was already on its way over there. As the day drew to a close, friends and neighbors said their goodbyes, each of them clinging to Eli for a few extra seconds with their hugs and handshakes unsure of what to say to someone going to his second war in just two years.

We spent the holiday with family then left the next day for a vacation in northern Georgia. We had planned to go to our favorite beach location, Orange Beach, Alabama, but the devastating oil spill that began a few months earlier had essentially shut down the Gulf. I knew we needed to get away to make some memories, and based on the recommendation of a friend, we chose a large cabin that sat on top of a mountain overlooking the small town of Blue Ridge.

The next few days were spent rafting the Ocoee River just across the border in Tennessee, riding horses (I watched while they rode), hanging out at the cabin, and going out for dinner. Eli seemed to relax during our time there. It was different from our normal family vacation. New activities and surroundings made it special. In the backs of our minds, however, we knew the clock was ticking and each of us tried to bury the stress of his impending departure.

Since Eli first told us he wanted to be a United States Marine, we had hoped that he would somehow escape from serving in a war zone. Although we lived 750 miles from New York City at the time, our lives and the future course of our family was significantly altered by the events that unfolded on September 11, 2001. We were not alone in this regard. Thousands of children and teens from all walks of life and locations around the United States decided to step forward to serve their country when old enough.

The day before the attacks, Eli had been a carefree twelve-year-old kid who loved to ride his bike, play with his younger brother and the other kids in the neighborhood, and get into trouble periodically at school for being too social. He enjoyed being around people of all ages. In the days that followed 9/11, his entire focus shifted. He was deeply affected by the attack on our country. In an adult-like manner, he told us that he had decided to join the Marine Corps to fight for his country as soon as he finished high school. Obviously, at that time we couldn't have known that our country would fight two wars in the Middle East, nor could we have known that the wars in Iraq and Afghanistan would be ongoing years later.

Throughout the remainder of his middle school and high school years, Eli never wavered in his desire to serve his country. He believed it was part of his heritage. Eli's paternal great-grandfather was career enlisted Army, serving in Europe during World War II, then in Korea, and eventually in Vietnam, where my father also served. His maternal grandfather had also served in the Army as a medic.

Liv and I had many discussions with Eli about other possible avenues of service. Each time, he told us that being an Infantry Marine was the only job he wanted. As parents, we grew more and more concerned as Eli's senior year of high school approached because the wars in Iraq and Afghanistan had dragged on for years. We felt like we were on a collision course with one or both wars that would cost us our son.

We played Devil's Advocate. We begged him to reconsider going to the Navy or the Coast Guard so that he wouldn't be part of the ground war. Nothing we said or did had any impact on Eli's eventual decision to follow through with the commitment he made to his country as a child. *His country*— that's how he thought of it. He realized it was *our country*, but by thinking of it as his, he claimed ownership and responsibility for its well-being.

"The Few, The Proud ... The Marines." Each military branch has a culture of its own, but none is more identifiable than the Marine Corps. During Eli's senior year, as a family we went through our own version of an indoctrination program. We read and talked about Marine Corps history, customs, and ethos. We learned the meaning of the terms "grunt," "leatherneck," and "jarhead." We immersed ourselves in the culture of the Marine Corps in much the same way the parents of a college student would a university before arriving for the first day of classes. Three weeks after graduation from high school, Eli left for Basic Training. He earned his Eagle, Globe, and Anchor and became a United States Marine in September 2007.

The seventeenth day of July 2010 was a gorgeous one on the North Carolina coast. Our family left our hotel in Jacksonville and met Eli at Camp Lejeune. We arrived at a large parking lot that resembled a pregame tailgate. Families and groups of people sat on truck tailgates or in folding chairs around coolers filled with water and soft drinks. Couples lay on blankets in the grassy areas surrounding the parking lot near the water's edge. A few canopy tents were set up near one end of the lot serving burgers, hotdogs, chips, and drinks. Large, desert tan duffels and other gear were piled in large groups nearest the road. Hundreds of Marines in their desert digi-cammies were among the groups, families, and couples. Many of them held small children or babies. The day had the feel of an enormous family reunion.

Eli led us around the parking lot and introduced us to a few of his closest buddies and their families, never staying in one spot for more than a few minutes as to not intrude on the precious time they shared before they parted ways. We settled near a dock on the bay that bordered the lot. Conversation was minimal as we had already said what we needed to over the past couple weeks.

Images of that day are what I remember most, like looking at a photo album that exists only in my mind: images of the newborn, then the toddler; of the first day of school, then on the baseball field; of long hair and rebellion, then the incredible man he had become. I remember Max's interactions with Eli—unsure of what to say, and unsure of how to deal with his emotions—knowing it could be the last few moments he would ever spend with his big brother. I remember watching Eli as he paced the dock, looking out at the shimmering waves with a faraway look. He was ready to get on with it while we were clinging to every second. I remember watching Liv try to come to terms with our son leaving, not knowing if this would be the last time we would see him. I understood how she felt, as memories of our boy's life flooded my thoughts. It was as if someone had torn through my flesh, reached into my chest, and was slowly, unmercifully tearing out my heart.

Stress was the trigger that released the irritated monster from its cage, and try as I might to fight it, the monster made its presence known outwardly. I couldn't hide it as my body showed the signs of the turmoil inside me. I just hoped I wouldn't become completely unglued before Eli departed. I didn't want him worry about me any more than he did already.

The few hours we had together went by too quickly, and we knew our time together was up when the buses arrived. We blended into the sea of the soon to be left behind and the young Marines with stern faces as we moved toward the buses. The Marines separated into their companies for formation as we watched. The buses were soon loaded with their gear, and it was finally time. Everyone scrambled to get one last hug, kiss, and an "I love you" before they disappeared one by one into the buses with windows so dark they couldn't be seen behind the glass. It was the last time that several families would see their loved ones alive.

The buses pulled out as we and the other families waved small American flags and cheered for our Marines as they willingly departed for hell on earth. It was as if being forced to inhale and unable to exhale, so similar to the day many years before when the thought of losing Eli overwhelmed us for the first time. The passage of time slowed significantly in that moment, as if an unseen slow-motion button had been engaged. Once the buses were out of sight, I began the long, slow walk to our car. It was the longest walk of my life, and one of the hardest things I've ever done: taking those steps toward the future, not knowing if I would ever see my son again.

13

GET UP AND WALK

Out of my distress I called on the Lord;
the Lord answered me and set me free.

PSALM 118:5, ESV

The normal gestation period from conception to birth for a human is approximately forty weeks. In my unusual case, it took only sixty-eight days from conception to the birth of my new life. September 22, 2010, became my Alive Day. Most often, the term *Alive Day* is used by those in the military who survive a horrible event that left them alive but with permanent injuries. It's the day one should have died, but didn't. In general, it can mean the day that one comes to a literal fork in life's road—one path leads to death, the other to a new life. Nothing is ever the same as it was before that day and that choice.

The decision was spiritual and instinctual. Live or die, fight for a life worth living, a life with purpose, or continue withering away to nothing. I crossed over a line that day when

I began the process of not only reclaiming the life I had before Parkinson's disease and the devastation it had brought into my life, but also a better life that included all of the lessons learned from eight long years of struggle.

I couldn't have imagined the things that God would do in my life, or all I would do or see in the future. It had taken years, but I finally let go of all I had lost, realizing that none of it had ever really mattered. My focus was on what I had yet to lose, the only thing on this earth that had mattered all along and that which had kept me tethered to life throughout the most difficult of times: my family.

Although I had felt uneasy most of the time while Eli was in Iraq, I was worried sick every minute he was in Afghanistan. The troop surge that Eli's unit was part of seemed to instigate more fighting in Taliban strongholds. Casualties increased considerably. Weeks at a time would pass with no communication with Eli, so we searched for as much information as we could find online, since most television media appeared to have forgotten the ongoing war in Afghanistan. Brave young men were injured or killed almost daily, yet hardly a word was mentioned by the American media. It was if the wars had ended but no one had told those who serve and their families.

Eli's best friend and stateside roommate is a fellow 2/9 Echo Company Marine by the name of Kyle. During a conversation between the two that took place several months before deploying to Afghanistan, Eli shared his concerns about me and my struggles with Parkinson's disease. Kyle's reply stunned Eli. His father was also battling Parkinson's. They had known each other for more than a year, but neither had known this about the other. They resolved to remedy the situation and introduce their fathers to one another before deploying to Afghanistan.

Sam and Nancy, Kyle's father and mother, live with their younger children in north Texas. We met by phone and were amazed by how much we have in common. During our sons' deployment to Afghanistan, we relied heavily on each other to make sense of our lives and similar struggles. Who else could understand exactly what the other was going through on a daily basis? Both of us were fighting Parkinson's while our sons were fighting the Taliban in Afghanistan. God's hand in providing support for both of us was unmistakable.

Several times a day, I reviewed an online casualty reporting website for Operation Enduring Freedom, the formal name for the war in Afghanistan. The casualty reporting website would show the date of death, unit, and location where the death occurred, but would show "Name Not Released Yet" pending notification of next of kin.

I'm not sure what most families of other servicemembers in Iraq and Afghanistan did to ease their anxiety, but I needed to know if I should be expecting the knock at the front door and finding Marines in their dress blues upon opening it. Each time I saw a new death, or KIA, reported in Helmand Province, I would hold my breath until I knew it wasn't Eli. Until I knew otherwise, every phone call, knock at the door, ring of the doorbell, or the sight of nondescript sedan gave me a sense of heart-sickening dread and I instantaneously became more symptomatic. When a name other than Eli's would appear, I felt the rush of the conflicting emotions of relief and guilt/sorrow. Relief that it wasn't Eli and guilt and sorrow that another family had received the news that their loved one wasn't coming home.

Living this way day after day nearly drove me insane. There was no relief from the torment of not knowing if I would ever see my son again. My soul ached not knowing from one minute to the next if Eli was alive, and it was smothering the barely smoldering embers of what strength I had left.

Our family closed ranks and developed tunnel vision. Nothing else in the world mattered to us except the welfare of our family. Washington, D.C. could have burned to the ground, California could have fallen into the Pacific Ocean, or all the people in New York City could have vanished overnight and we wouldn't have known. The only news we sought was to know if our son was alive and well. Liv and I rarely spoke about it, or we would be brought to tears of desperation before we could get more than a few words out. We knew it consumed most of our waking thoughts, so we hugged often and focused on moments with Max to bring us a few fleeting moments of joy.

We tried to keep busy with mundane daily tasks, and preparing and shipping care packages for Eli. We knew he would share with other Marines, so we shipped as many as we could afford. The greatest day we could experience was one in which we spoke to Eli, even if for only a few minutes. The joy would begin to subside the next day because the uncertainty and waiting would begin anew, knowing it could be weeks before we heard from him.

Parkinson's can wreak havoc on sleep, so I was in a restless state between being awake and asleep when I received a call from Eli in the early hours of a September morning. It had been weeks since we last heard from him. Since the day he left for Afghanistan, my phone was on and within arm's reach on a 24/7 basis, as I never knew when he would call, and I couldn't bear the thought of missing the chance to hear his voice.

As soon as he began talking, I knew he wasn't in a good place. He asked how I was and how his mom and Max were doing. He wanted to talk yet didn't say much, so I pressed him to tell me what was on his mind. Eli's unit had been in the Marjah district of Afghanistan for six weeks and had already suffered four casualties: one Navy Corpsman in an accident and three Marines killed in action.

Eli was close personal friends with the two most recent fatalities, a fellow Lance Corporal and his team leader, a Corporal whom Eli respected and admired greatly. He spoke fondly of both young men, yet his overall tone was one of detachment. In a matter-of-fact way, he told me that he believed that he wasn't meant to make it home from Afghanistan.

He needed to go through the process of mourning for his brother Marines, but his training and his mind were overruling his heart and suppressing the mourning process in order to focus on his job, and to keep himself and his fellow Marines alive. Eli had been tasked to assume the role of team leader left vacant with the death of his Corporal.

We talked for a few more minutes about seemingly inconsequential things—his way of avoiding the issue—before I woke Liv so she could hear his voice. I lay in bed listening to her side of the conversation and heard the subtle desperation in her voice while talking about anything to keep Eli on the line for a few more minutes, never knowing if it would be the last time we heard his voice.

After we said our goodbyes, I couldn't sleep and went to our home office to check email and send a message to my mom, brothers, and Sam that we had heard from Eli. I then pulled up the online casualty report and stared at the names on the long list of those who had made the ultimate sacrifice, specifically focusing on the names of the two men who were Eli's close friends.

Deep in the night, I shed tears for the young Corporal and Lance Corporal and for my son's broken heart. His words of resignation and acceptance regarding what he believed would be his end haunted me. It was then that I tried bargaining with God. I was willing to die in my son's place if only he would be allowed to live. On my knees, I begged God to not take my son from me, and I have no doubt He spoke to my heart that night.

I begged God for some peace, for some small token of re-assurance that we would make it through this. Try as I might, for most of my life I have felt like I'm spiritually deficient when it comes to understanding whatever it is that God wants me to do. I often think of myself as a spiritual Forrest Gump. As a Christian, I envy those who say that God speaks clearly to them. On many occasions, I have wished God would send an e-mail, or a Facebook message, or a Tweet, or a text message, or even a telegram telling me what it is I am to do. Whatever it is, I'll do it because it is my earnest desire.

As I've grown older and have become more honest with myself about who I am, I realize it probably has more to do with God knowing exactly how to lead me. He knows I can be profoundly focused on the task at hand and lose my need for direction until the job is finished. By only giving me bits of information, I must seek Him and His direction every step of the way. When He wants to make something absolutely clear to me, though, He always does so in a way that leaves zero room for doubt.

It's hard to describe to most people what I experienced on my knees that night while begging for my son's life. All I know is what happened in my soul. God gave me something that night, just as He had many years before when I was just a child. He gave me direction, and it was as clear to me as if He had spoken the command aloud.

If a transcript of that silent conversation between God and me existed, it would read something like this:

> **Me:** Dear God, please take me instead of Eli. My life has no value, and I would willingly surrender it to spare his.
>
> *God: You do know it doesn't work like that, right?*
>
> **Me:** (feeling appropriately chastised): I know. I know. But I don't know what else to do.
>
> *God: You trust Me, right?*
>
> **Me:** Well, of course.
>
> *God: Then, do as I say. Get up and walk.*
>
> **Me:** (feeling exasperated): Um, God, I know You know all, but do you see these legs? They haven't worked right in years. Besides, what does me walking have to do with saving Eli?
>
> *God: Do I really need to tell you again?*

Me: No, Lord. I just don't understand. Why is it so important that I walk?

God: *You need to meet your son where he will be.*

I need to meet Eli where he will be? What does that mean? Although I didn't understand, I believed I would see my son again. Hope overpowered despair that night. I didn't know if he would return home wounded, or how he would need me, but the command had been written indelibly on my soul. I needed to have the will to not only fight to stay alive, but also to become more than I had been in several years, perhaps more than I had ever been.

Just as a newborn has no cognitive awareness that the day he left his mother's womb and entered this world is, in fact, his birthday, I wasn't aware of just how definitive the line I had crossed was. I didn't understand that my new life had been born, and I didn't know that I would soon take my first steps toward freedom from my inescapable prison. All I could think about was obeying the command I had been given: *Get up and walk.*

14

LINE IN THE SAND

Not till we are completely lost or turned around...
do we begin to find ourselves.

HENRY DAVID THOREAU

A s I was going through my early life finding success in most things I set out to do—sports, education, marriage, family, and career—I often marveled at how others could fail so completely. Whether it is the alcoholic like my father, the drug addict, the sex addict, the gambling addict, or the whatever-addict, I couldn't understand why people had to fail so miserably before doing something to attempt a comeback. Why couldn't they make a mistake and rebound before completely shattering their lives and their family's lives into a million pieces? Why did people have to hit rock bottom before doing something about it? After traveling such a difficult road since, I marvel at how I could have had so little empathy for the struggles people face and the obstacles they can't overcome on their own without some help.

I would love to go back in time and have a "come to Jesus" meeting with the man I was then. I would give him some knowledge that would humble him and rock his world to the core. Unfortunately, that's not how things work. The man I used to be—confident to the point of arrogance, emotionally tough, and physically and mentally strong—had faded into a memory, worn down by mental fatigue and the overwhelming physical, emotional, and spiritual pain. The beaten down man I had become was preparing the white flag of surrender. I had reached a point in life where I was so tired of the suffering and so drained of hope, and had accepted that a fast-approaching death was imminent, and to be honest, welcomed at times.

I have always been willing to die for my wife and children, and I believe most people feel the same way about their families. But was I willing to live for them? Was I willing to not just survive, but fight to live even if it meant more suffering than I had already endured? After my heart-to-heart with God the September night Eli called and told me to prepare for the worst, I was ready to do whatever it took to live and to be wherever, whenever Eli would need me.

Several months before Eli deployed to Afghanistan, my primary care physician suggested that I have bariatric surgery to aid in reducing my weight with the hope that several of my health conditions could be lessened in severity. At Liv's urging, I had jumped through the medical and insurance hoops in preparation for the surgery, but I had been reluctant to follow through because I felt hopeless. Once I made the decision to take action, though, things moved swiftly.

The team of doctors I saw for treatment of Parkinson's and the other ailments that had accumulated over the eight years since my health problems began, worked together to help me move forward in a new direction. They quickly arrived at the conclusion that an adjustable gastric band was the best option. I needed to keep my digestive system intact for future Parkinson's drug treatment options, including the possibility that I may someday need an intestinal pump medication delivery system.

Honestly, I didn't care—just pick the most viable option and go with it. I had somewhere I needed to be, and needed a little help to get there. I was cautioned the surgery wasn't a quick fix and that most patients who underwent gastric band surgery could expect to lose just enough weight to get medical conditions under control provided the nutrition plan was followed and specific behavioral changes were incorporated. They had no idea how motivated I was or how I planned to exceed their expectations by meeting my own.

When I went to UAB Hospital the morning of the surgery, I didn't go there for cosmetic reasons or because my doctors said I needed to do it. I wasn't doing this for me. I was there for Eli and for Max and Liv. By submitting to the surgeon's scalpel, I knew I was crossing a line in the sand. It was just the first step in a process that would enable me to take the next one, then the next. No matter how difficult the process would be, I didn't plan on returning to the desolate place of despair I was leaving behind.

After I woke in the recovery room, I felt like I had barely survived an evisceration. For me, the pain was an unmistakable road sign that I was heading in a new direction. It was pain that I had chosen to endure in order to pass through to the other side. In those first few hours after waking from surgery, I had to remind myself several times that pain can have purpose.

Near midnight, I asked the nurse to help me out of bed so I could move around some. A short time later, I was outside the hospital room doing a few extremely slow laps around the corridors in my hospital gown. Sweat beaded on my forehead from the effort as I shuffled while also touching the walls for balance. The night shift nurses at their station must have wondered where the stooped over, pudgy man was going in the middle of the night with the look on his face of a runner who had hit the wall at the twenty-mile mark, but who was determined to finish the race.

15

TEN MILE ROCK

Sometimes I lie awake at night, and ask,
"Where have I gone wrong?"
Then a voice says to me,
"This is going to take more than one night."

CHARLES M. SCHULZ

O ur former neighborhood in a suburb of Birmingham, Alabama, stretches over 1,400 acres of forested hills with streets branching out along the ridge lines. Several small man-made lakes were created in the valleys when the property was developed. Swimming isn't allowed, but the lakes are stocked with fish and are a haven for lone fishermen trying to find a few moments of peace after a long work day. Families with small children frequent the edges of the lakes during weekends, and people in canoes and kayaks rowing for exercise are common in the spring and summer months.

A natural walking/jogging trail was constructed around the most easily accessible lake across from the neighborhood activity center. The twists and turns of the trail measure exactly three-quarters of a mile from start to finish, and it was a beautiful place to begin what would soon become *The Walk*.

On that early October morning, I stood at the trailhead beside my truck, my hand touching it for balance. I left my cane and my leg brace at home, roughly half a mile from where I stood looking out at the mist that hovered above the still water in the early morning light. It was the day I had been anticipating during the brief recovery from surgery. At just after daybreak, I took my first steps on the lake trail, steps that would lead me to where my son needed me to be when he returned home from war, and eventually to Mt. Kilimanjaro.

Love is the greatest motivator in my life. Since the day Liv and I became one, love is what tips the scales one way or the other. Every decision I make is weighed against how it affects Liv, Eli, and Max. From successes and mistakes along the way, I have learned that taking steps in a new direction will have consequences and long-lasting, far-reaching ripple effects. The first step is always the hardest. On this day, I knew with certainty I was going in the right direction.

I had grown so accustomed to using the cane and leg brace that the first hundred yards or so without them were wobbly and uncertain on the uneven earthen trail. I shuffled several hundred feet at a time, my left arm involuntarily still by my side, and my right arm moving in exaggerated arcs to compensate. My head was down in the stooped posture like many with Parkinson's as I focused on each step. Without the use of the walking aids, I was learning to walk again.

When I stopped to rest, I could feel the dull ache in my abdomen. Carrying nearly three hundred pounds on a frame meant to support less than two hundred didn't help matters much. I repeated the process several times until I had circumnavigated the lake and reached the point where I had started. Time to complete the first lap: just under an hour.

The effort had taken everything I had to complete it. I understood my exact starting point on the journey with an unknown destination. I was standing at the bottom of a terribly deep hole at the base of an extremely tall mountain. I thought about a phrase I heard Eli repeat often when referring to the parts of his job that he didn't enjoy but had to do nonetheless: *Embrace the suck.* Yes, this was going to hard, but I was determined to move forward.

I returned to the neighborhood lake trail every day for the next week determined to add distance each day, even if only a few feet. The routine was the same with my head down focusing on my next shuffle step, one arm not moving and the other in an exaggerated three-quarter windmill motion. I tried to focus on just completing the circuit around the lake, but the thought that encompassed all others was that I was moving toward a destination where I would meet my son.

Over the course of that first week, I began to think of my time on the trail as walking with Eli on patrol but on opposite sides of the world. I prayed for his protection with each step I took. I knew the walks made no difference for him in the physical sense, but believed what I was doing made a difference in a spiritual sense. The bond between parent and child transcends the explainable. Eli would know I had his back.

I had been so focused on the next step in front of me and thinking about Eli that I had noticed little of my surroundings while on the trail. When I finally stopped to take stock of my progress, I noticed an enormous rock outcropping on the other side of the lake. I had walked past it several times, but hadn't really noticed it. It was the only natural part along the edge of the man-made lake, so large it hadn't been moved by the machinery that had cleared the valley and built the dam to hold the water. Intrigued, I picked up the pace, which was negligible at best, and made my way to the other side of the lake to have a closer look.

When I came to the rock, I started to step up on it for a better view of the lake and surroundings, but as I approached the rock I stopped. Men had cut trees and moved tons of dirt and smaller rocks to make this lake, but either had been unable to move this large rock or someone decided it wasn't worth the effort. Everything else in this large neighborhood had been sculpted, manicured, or made by someone, yet the rock remained steadfast in its place, unmoved by and impervious to the whims of man.

I realized I didn't deserve to stand on the rock—not yet, anyway. Most who passed by the rock on their walks around the small lake were probably indifferent to it and rarely, if ever, gave it a moment of thought. For me though, it was as if the rock had been placed in this spot ages ago waiting for me, waiting to motivate me, waiting to physically represent something spiritual.

I was drawn to the big rock. I found a spot to sit just off the trail and focused on it. The motivation to become something more than I had been able to be for most of the years my sons grew from children into men only intensified. A seed planted long ago began to grow and take shape into something that would change my whole outlook, and enable me to finally get a glimpse of what God had been doing through the years of suffering.

I don't recall where I first heard the story, but it had stuck with me for a reason. As I sat there looking at the rock, I got the message of the story in a whole new light.

One night, a man was awakened when he felt the presence of someone in his room. He opened his eyes, and was surprised to see Jesus standing beside his bed. "Don't be troubled," Jesus said. "I have a job for you. When you wake in the morning, go outside. There you will find a large rock. I want you to push on it."

When the man woke in the morning, he thought he must have been dreaming. When he walked outside, he found a boulder large enough to cast a shadow over his home. An obedient man, he did as Jesus had told him ... he began pushing on the rock.

Day after day, he pushed on the rock from sunrise until sunset. He tried many ways to move the rock, but the rock never moved. Days became months, and months became years. He never asked why Jesus had chosen him to push on the rock or why it was necessary, but over time he became frustrated because the rock never moved. He was almost ready to give up.

One night, the man was once again awakened by the presence of someone in his room. When he opened his eyes, he saw Jesus standing beside his bed. Jesus said. "Tell me what troubles you."

"I have done as you told me, but the rock doesn't move," the man said. "I have failed, and I don't understand why you have given me such an impossible task."

Smiling, Jesus placed His hand on the man's shoulder. Reassuring him, He began to explain, "Day after day, you have done as I asked. Look at your skin—it is able to withstand the elements like never before. Look at your body—every muscle, ligament, and tendon has been pushed to its limit and forced to grow stronger. Look at your mind—you have thought of many ways to push the rock, and your mind has grown and become focused like never before. You are ready."

The man still didn't fully understand and asked, "Ready for what? I didn't move the rock."

"I asked you to push the rock, not to move it," Jesus replied. "Moving the rock is my job. Now you are ready for what comes next."

I was overwhelmed by the epiphany and the life-altering shift in how I look at living with Parkinson's disease. For the first time since Parkinson's entered my life, I had some spiritual insight into what I believe to be God's purpose for my struggle: It was meant to make me strong in my relationship with Him and to prepare me to fulfill His purpose for my life.

Many times I had felt like Sisyphus, damned for the remainder of my life to push a rock uphill again and again as punishment for my hubris. Somehow this rock and the lesson God would teach me through it played a role in His plan and the direction my life would take. I could see but a few steps in front of me on the path I was now on, but I knew I was heading in the right direction. I had no idea what challenges lay ahead of me on my journey, but I was determined to push harder on the rock than ever before and trust that it would make me stronger and that it would be moved when the time was right.

Standing on the rock became the first goal, and it would eventually become my first summit. I would not stand on top of the rock until I could walk ten miles in one day, which was a daunting task considering my present condition. I named it Ten Mile Rock. The laps around the lake trail had purpose before, but now I had a tangible mental and physical goal to work toward, albeit far beyond my grasp at the time. Each time I felt the crushing despair of not knowing what was happening with Eli, I was given the same answer. Keep moving forward toward the time and place where I would see my son again. *Push the rock.*

16

KILIMANJARO:
DAY 1 - TO MACHAME CAMP

24 AUG 2012

The first two miles of the Machame Route are on a wide trail, wide enough to allow 4WD vehicles to traverse its course. As the group took our first steps on the trail, we were excited to finally start the actual climb to the summit of Mt. Kilimanjaro. I stopped to take a quick photo of the simple wooden sign with the words, "Starting Point, Machame Route, wishing you a good climb," engraved in all caps and painted yellow on brown-colored wood. It was official. I was no longer planning for the climb, or on a plane or a bus, or mere feet from the trail waiting for the green light to begin. I was actually on the trail that would lead me to complete the discovery of who I had become.

As the trail gradually narrowed and weaved its way into the tall trees and lush vegetation of the cloud forest, we transitioned from walking in a pack to hiking in a single-file line with Steven leading the way. Purposefully, I allowed other members of the group to move ahead of me. Not that I needed to be at the back of the line. It's where I wanted to be. In the years since diagnosis, I had become accustomed to moving slower than others and it had taught me about the things I had missed before Parkinson's entered my life. It taught me how to be led and how to experience other people in the moment.

As the oldest child in my family, I was thrust into a leadership role from birth. I thought it was my responsibility to be out front, blazing trails for my younger brothers, then later for my own family. When "walking point," the focus is on the environment that lies before me, looking for pitfalls and the dangers, always seeking the best direction to go. Unfortunately, it's easy to miss out on being in the company of those behind me on the path.

In its own way, Parkinson's had taken my hand and led me to the rear of the pack over the years. Sometimes, it was out of physical necessity as my body did not allow me to move with the speed or precision I had known for the first thirty-six years of my life. Many times, it was because I had no idea where the disease was taking me, and I had no choice but to stumble about until I came upon some kind of trail marker to show me the way.

The slow process of moving from walking point to bringing up the rear had allowed me to move through life with a different perspective. It allowed for many opportunities to meet others where they are on their journey, and to truly get to know the grace, compassion, and goodness of those I encounter.

I listened to the conversations of my teammates as we moved slowly up the trail. The bits and pieces I picked up on of their stories about what brought them to Kilimanjaro were intriguing. Most of the words spoken were about others who faced much tougher obstacles than what lay before us on this mountain. Love, compassion, and empathy had provided the motivation to come to this place, and powered their every step upward. As the group settled into the slow rhythm of the hike, Tyler, my hiking buddy, and I talked about places we had hiked in preparation for the climb and what brought us to make this trek. Although we had come together on this mountain from two different places in life, we found common ground quickly.

An hour or so into the climb, we stopped for a brief break where the wide trail narrows significantly. The tall trees and the dense vegetation formed a canopy over us. Our environment was foreign to us in nearly every way, from the language we heard spoken by our Tanzanian counterparts to the trees, plants, and even the dirt beneath our feet.

When we began hiking again, I had an unexpected urge to move to the front of the line just behind Steven. I wanted to move more quickly up the trail toward our first camp, and hoped that moving to the front of the group would make it so. However, it didn't take long to become frustrated with Steven's slow, steady steps. I nearly stepped on his feet several times as I tried not to fall into a trance by the rhythm of his slow, nearly hypnotic movements.

After an hour or so of frustration, I stepped out of line, acting as if I needed to adjust something on my pack and was ready to go again just as the end of the line passed by me. Once again, I was reminded that Kilimanjaro operates on its own time and at its own pace.

As we slowly plodded along, Steven allowed the members of the group to acclimatize to the rise in elevation. He knew what he was doing, and he would not modify his approach to quell the impatience of anyone in the group. Since more than half of the population of the United States lives in coastal regions, it is safe to assume that the majority of Americans who come to climb Kilimanjaro live well below the elevation of the starting point of our climb.

Nearly everyone in our group lived at or below 1,000 feet elevation, and had been in Africa for less than thirty-six hours. A few of those who had come from New York had been in country for a little more than twelve hours at the start of the climb. With only minimal time to acclimate to the elevation of Arusha (approximately 4,500 feet) before the climb began, we moved upward with each step from the starting point elevation of approximately 5,942 feet at the Machame Gate toward the Machame Camp at 9,911 feet (Stedman, 2010, p. 266).

The air in the earth's atmosphere contains approximately 21% oxygen, 78% nitrogen, and 1% other gases. The air contains the same percentages of gases at the summit of Mt. Kilimanjaro as it does at sea level. However, as one moves up the mountain, the density of air changes and it becomes thinner. There are fewer oxygen molecules in the air at high altitude as a result of the decrease in atmospheric pressure.

At around 8,000 feet the air has approximately 75% of the oxygen available at sea level, and climbers who are susceptible may begin to show signs of altitude sickness. Upon reaching the location of our first camp, the air will have approximately 70% of the oxygen available at sea level, and at the summit the air will have slightly less than half of the oxygen available at sea level. This is why Steven was moving so slowly, especially on the first day of the climb.

We heard *pole pole* many times from Steven, his assistant guides, and the porters from the groups behind us on the trail as they passed us carrying gear, tents, food and other necessities. Pronounced, "po-lay, po-lay," it is Swahili for, "slowly, slowly."

I didn't need to acclimatize like the others, but I understood the process. I had been living in Colorado at 7,200 feet for several months, and had trained at elevations up to 14,440 feet in preparation for climbing Kilimanjaro. The elevation of the first day was similar to the areas where I went for my frequent training hikes in Colorado.

For the first time in a decade, I had a physical advantage, albeit small when weighed against the fitness levels and youth of my counterparts. The increase in red blood cells to carry oxygen to my muscles and increased lung capacity from living and training at altitude were just two of the many rewards I had received from my time in the Rockies.

Several times, I had to resist the urge to run the rest of the way to camp, but I was part of a group, part of a team. Besides, I hadn't run in years. I wasn't quite at that level yet, but the yearning was there. Although I had thought about this scenario several times beforehand, once out on the trail my competitive spirit and sheer excitement about what I was now capable of doing took over. It took a few hours, but I was able to quell the independent and competitive parts of my nature and settle into the rhythm of the team effort. After so much time spent alone on my journey, I relished being part of a team again. As the team went, so did I.

The total distance from the Machame Gate to Machame Camp is a little more than six miles. We stopped for lunch at the halfway point, and we needed the break, not so much because we were tired, but to break up the monotony of the trek through the rain forest. The initial excitement of the day was beginning to wane. One can be surrounded by tall trees and dense vegetation for only so long before becoming bored. We could see no more than thirty yards in front or behind us at any given time. On the trail for several hours, we hadn't caught even a glimpse of Kibo, the tallest, newest, and most recognizable of Kilimanjaro's three volcanic cones (Mawenzi and Shira are the other two). I had anticipated that the first day of climbing would be monotonous in comparison to the remaining days, and had found it to be true so far.

By the time we stopped for lunch break, most of us had consumed between one and two liters of water from our hydration bladders or Nalgene bottles. Hydration is one of the most important parts of acclimatizing at high altitude in order to avoid the onset, or worsening, of acute mountain sickness (AMS). We pulled the box lunches from our packs and soon got our first taste of the food we would have while on the mountain. I skipped the butter sandwich (as did most of the group) and went straight to the small, cold meat pie fritter. The brown boiled egg and the fruit were eaten quickly as well, washed down with the lukewarm fruit juice. With the first meal on the mountain gone, I was glad I had brought several days' supply of both protein and energy bars to supplement the meals.

After lunch, the trek upward continued in much the same fashion it had before. My first glimpse of Kibo came within an hour of reaching camp. Through the trees to our right, the square, glacier-topped peak appeared. We snapped photos of our eventual destination, and the sight of it gave the group a much needed bump in motivation.

As we drew closer to camp, the trees became shorter and the vegetation less dense until the forest opened up into a slightly sloped clearing where our tents were set up for the night. Kibo was now clearly visible to the east, as was Mt. Meru to the southwest. At just shy of 10,000 feet, we were well above the cloud cover that rolled like the sea to the horizon. It was as if the African savanna didn't exist below the sea of clouds and I was on a mountain island.

It had been a long day, starting early at the hotel, traveling by bus to Kilimanjaro National Park, navigating the registration process, and then hiking through the cloud forest. The first day of the five-day ascent was drawing to a close. Darkness descended upon us while the group crowded inside the meal tent. Everyone was tired, but happy about reaching camp where warm drinks and food awaited us.

Throughout the day, the group didn't fracture into cliques or subgroups, which is rare for a group so large. As I looked around the makeshift, candle-lit dining table, I realized that this was not just a great group of people. We had all of the necessary ingredients required to be an exceptional team.

The meal was served in stages. First, hot water for tea, coffee, or the favorite of most groups who traverse Kilimanjaro, Milo, a chocolate and malt powder that can be mixed with hot or cold water (although it's much better when served hot). The soup was served next, and was glorious in comparison to what we had consumed for much of the day. With chicken broth as its base, a sprinkling of vegetables was added. The main course was heavy on carbohydrates with small portions of meat. The pre-meal drinks and the soup were meant to rehydrate, and the carb-rich meal at the end of the day was provided to restore and build up energy for the continuation of the climb in the morning.

During the main course, Will proposed that we begin a ritual that would continue for the duration of our time on Kilimanjaro. One by one, each member of the group made a brief statement about a bad thing and a good thing that happened or was observed that day. Everyone had trouble coming up with a bad thing, and had multiple good things to choose from to discuss. As we went in turn around the table, it became an opportunity for everyone to show a bit of their personalities, as in who was shy, who were the jokesters, who were deep thinkers. We laughed often, and it was a great team bonding activity. It lifted my spirits higher than they were already.

After the dinner meal and before entering my tent, I stood alone looking at the moonlit peak of Kilimanjaro and listened to the faint chatter in the porters' tents across the clearing. The warm, tropical day had transitioned to a cool, bordering on cold, night on the mountain at more than double the elevation of Arusha. Still and silent, I watched as, one by one, headlamps were extinguished inside the tents around the camp. This is where I was meant to be.

17

BROTHERS-IN-ARMS

It's like deja vu, all over again.

Yogi Berra

We knew the day was coming at some point. We were resigned to it. We expected it. And when it came, there was no other choice than to give him our support. During the same period of time Eli was in Afghanistan, Max was in the first semester of his senior year of high school. At times, it seemed unfair for Max to be experiencing what should be *his year* while our family was so focused on the dangers Eli faced every day.

Although he had many things going on in his own life, Max remained focused on the family by showing his strength and maturity in the way he supported Liv and me. He had decisions of his own to make about his future, but didn't feel the need to talk things over with us. Like me, he works the puzzle in his mind, considering options and narrowing his mental pros and cons list before seeking input. Unlike me yet so much like Liv, he doesn't talk about the decision-making process until it is completed. Only then does he inform others regarding his intentions.

College seemed to be far down the priority list. Liv and I had pressed him at times during the latter part of the summer before school began for something definitive regarding his plans, but he was either noncommittal or didn't want to share what was going on inside his head. That changed during the fall. Whether he had known for some time, or if Eli's deployment to Afghanistan had bearing on his decision, he wouldn't tell. As if one child being in harm's way as a member of the Marine Corps wasn't enough, when Max proclaimed that he intended to become a Marine after high school ended, Liv and I had the same thought: Here we go again.

The Marine Corps has our deepest respect and admiration. They are highly trained warfighters, plain and simple, and are among the finest men and women our country has to offer. Far too many Marines have died in Iraq and Afghanistan. Our older son was in the midst of combat almost daily at the time, and now our younger son was about to follow a similar path. From the viewpoint of a parent though, it was a tough pill to swallow. We feared for Eli's life every hour of the day and night. Did Liv and I have it in us to live with that fear for both of our children? We didn't have a choice.

A sense of duty and fairness led us to attempt a similar process with Max as we had with Eli. Since Liv and I had been through this once before, we knew the progression of events that would soon come to pass. Max had learned from watching how things had played out over time with Eli, so we knew he was serious when he stated clearly that he had no patience for the questions. Although he understood our concerns, Max knew what he wanted and was determined to move forward with his plans. Our parental hopes hinged on United States troops being out of Afghanistan before Max made it to the fleet, and that he would have a long, peacetime career in the United States Marine Corps.

18

WINTER BLANKETS

Not only that, but we rejoice in our sufferings,
knowing that suffering produces endurance,
and endurance produces character,
and character produces hope.

ROMANS 5:3-4, ESV

The men of 2d Battalion, 9th Marines, operated out of a Forward Operating Base, or FOB, on the outskirts of the Marjah district in Helmand Province. Multiple FOBs were located several kilometers apart and 15-25 kilometers from and encircling the Main Operating Base near the center of the Marjah district. Marines occupied buildings or compounds that had been taken from the Taliban. Most of the buildings were little more than primitive mud huts with rough openings and no windows or doors, fortified by an exterior perimeter barrier with entry control points. The FOBs were remote outposts under constant threat of attack by the Taliban.

Winter was approaching quickly in Afghanistan. The scorching, triple digit temperature days of summer had transitioned to bearable temperatures in the 80s during the day and 50s at night. But it would soon get much colder. It was mid-October when I heard Eli's voice on the other end of the line.

It had been nearly three weeks since his last call, and it was good to hear his voice. He asked about how the surgery had gone and what I was allowed to eat. I shared that eating wasn't part of my current vocabulary as I was still on a post-surgery liquid diet. It didn't matter though, because I was excited to share with him that I had dropped thirty pounds in the first three weeks following surgery, quickly meeting the weight loss goal my physicians had established prior. I was more excited to tell him that I had walked three miles in a little more than an hour without the cane and leg brace the day before. He was happy for me, and it was good to hear the positivity in his voice.

He thanked me for sending care packages and said his family back in the States was becoming popular with the guys at the FOB as he shared everything with his fellow Marines. He declined to discuss anything about the fight against the Taliban because of operations security (OPSEC) concerns, but I suspected that he just didn't want to talk about how difficult the situation was and played the OPSEC card to avoid the subject. Since our last conversation, three additional 2/9 Marines had been killed in action bringing the total number of casualties to seven during the first three months of the seven-month deployment.

He spoke with his mother and brother before his allotted time on the satellite phone was up. Something he said

during our conversation stuck with me. Eli has always hated
cold weather. He endures it when necessary, but being a child
of the South he dreads winter in any location. He asked if
we would send him a blanket because he had to sleep fully
clothed beneath the standard-issued wool covering in an attempt to stay warm at night. It would get much colder during
the remainder of their deployment, which was expected to
end in February 2011.

As soon as the conversation with Eli ended, I was on my
way to the local superstores to buy a blanket or two to send
out in a care package the next day. I was excited to be able to
fulfill a need for my son. I've learned from several other military families that they long for some way they can help their
family member while deployed. Of course, some satisfaction is
gained from sending care packages with snacks and toiletries,
but there's always a desire to help in a more tangible way.

Drifting off to sleep that night, I felt good. I had heard
Eli's voice that day, which made all seem right in the world
for a brief moment. I was making progress in the right direction in regard to my health. Although the physical activity was
still a struggle, it felt incredible to be moving again and to be
outdoors for extended periods of time. It was in the twilight
between wakefulness and sleep that an idea bubbled to the
surface of my consciousness. It was a simple idea that could
mean something to many people.

While Liv prepared for work the next morning, I ran the
idea by her. We could send blankets, along with a personal
note, to each of the young men in Eli's squad. There were four
men per fire team, and three fire teams in a squad for a total
of twelve. She loved the idea, and so did Max when I ran the
idea by him to get his thoughts about it.

The idea grew as I went about the business of purchasing blankets during the morning. By the time Liv arrived home from work that day, I had a full scale plan of attack. We shouldn't stop at providing for a need for the eleven Marines Eli worked with every day, or his platoon, or his company. We shouldn't stop until every Marine in the battalion had a blanket to meet their physical need, but just as important, a personal note with each one to let them know the people at home hadn't forgotten about them while they served and fought at a lonely outpost in Afghanistan.

The number of blankets required to bring my idea to fruition had jumped from twelve that morning to more than a thousand by that evening. Although glad to see my excitement about something that benefitted Eli and the men he served with, Liv was mildly concerned about my sanity. We couldn't afford to buy the number of blankets needed, but I had a plan and intended to see it through.

For the next five weeks, I was a man on a mission. I walked the lake trail nearly every morning, and then spent the remainder of the day on a social media blitz and talking to local businessmen and women, civic organizations, and churches about the plan. I sent emails to everyone on my contact list and posted information about what I called the "2/9 Marine Corps blanket drive" on my personal social media page and on Marine Corps family group pages. I spread the information on sports message boards and alumni websites.

The response was overwhelming and more than I imagined possible. Donations began pouring in within forty-eight hours of getting the word out. Purchasing, individually packaging each blanket with a personal note, and preparing large boxes stuffed with blankets for shipment became a full-time adventure. Each box contained a letter explaining who the blankets were from (e.g., an alumni group, church, business, or individual) and their intended purpose. One especially generous couple from the Memphis area, whom I had never met, donated more than $1,200 to the effort.

The boxes were shipped several at a time to the battalion chaplain, whose responsibility it was to coordinate the distribution of goods meant for all Marines to each location. I imagined when the onslaught of boxes arrived at the makeshift office of the chaplain at the 2/9 Main Operating Base, their reception would be appreciated. I also had little doubt the extra work created by a civilian was enough to probably make a military chaplain let go of some profanity.

The dining room in our home became a makeshift packaging and distribution center, which was quickly outgrown by the end of the first week. By the end of the second week, I had moved everything to the garage, where every inch of space was needed to accommodate the operation. During the day, I traveled throughout central Alabama and into Tennessee to buy blankets at every superstore I could locate. I left with an empty truck and returned late each afternoon with a full load. Had my neighbors not known what I was doing, they might have thought I was a doomsday prepper preparing for the end of civilization as we knew it.

There were people who donated by ordering online and shipping the blankets in large quantities directly to the 2/9 in Afghanistan, but the majority sent funds directly to me. I thought of it as a sacred responsibility to ensure that the funds were spent wisely and had the maximum intended effect. Liv and I reached deep into our available funds and paid for the most of the shipping costs ourselves. In just a little more than a month, dozens of individuals and organizations contributed to the effort, resulting in approximately $6,000 contributed and more than fifteen hundred blankets shipped to the 2/9 in Afghanistan.

The project exceeded the number of blankets required for each Marine to receive a small piece of home, with several hundred blankets in reserve for the next Marine battalion serving in that location the following winter. I personally handled eleven hundred blankets, and it was an honor and a privilege to serve the young men who sacrifice daily for the benefit of our country.

By the time the last shipment was sent, the first few shipments had arrived in Afghanistan and were being distributed. Eli had received the small boxes with the blankets for him and his squad, but didn't know the full extent of the project until he heard about it from Marines at other locations. Most didn't know the Lance Corporal's old man was involved, but Eli did.

Few career accomplishments made me feel as proud as did this small grass-roots project. The desire to do something for others had drawn me out of my isolation, forcing me back out into the world to connect with both people I knew and total strangers. I spoke to individuals and to large groups. I no longer cared if people noticed my physical differences. I had something I believed in and I gave it maximum effort. I learned that I still had something to contribute to the world to help make it a better place in some small way, and it sparked a passion within me for serving others. For the first time in years, I felt really alive.

19

KILIMANJARO:
DAY 2 - HAKUNA MATATA

25 AUG 2012

The day began with the sounds of movement outside our two-man tent. Tyler, much like my sons, could apparently sleep through Armageddon. Although I had fallen asleep quickly, I didn't sleep well throughout the night. Sleeping fully clothed in a sleeping bag on top of a thin pad wasn't the issue. Tyler and I had slept feet to head, and I realized I had slept with my head downhill when I felt the pressure from a sinus headache. It would probably linger for the remainder of the climb, but if it was the worst thing I had to deal with, I would count myself fortunate. Note to self: Choose a tent on more level ground next time.

Once outside the tent, the camp was a surprising model of efficiency. My teammates were rousing from their tents, brushing their teeth with water from their Nalgene bottles boiled the night before, making their morning visits to the bathroom tents, cleaning up with baby wipes, and readying their backpacks before making their way to the meal tent. Porters were breaking down tents and gathering the duffel bags of the climbers who had cast their bag into the pile to be carried up the mountain.

The cook's assistants were stopping at each tent to deliver coffee. To be honest, it was horrible. Some of my teammates raved about the bitter African brew, but I hated the stuff. It didn't matter though, because I crave caffeine as soon as my eyes open each morning. I downed a couple of cups, doing my best to ignore the taste and get the necessary kick start to begin the day.

Once again, the entire group of sixteen crowded into the tent for a meal. Breakfast began with fire pit-roasted toast. We sipped coffee or Milo while eating the toast, which we could top with a delicious natural peanut butter, jelly, or both, while waiting on the main course of porridge to arrive. A few teammates spoke of how surprised they were to have slept so well in a tent, while others looked like they had wrestled a bear during the night instead of sleeping. I belonged to the latter group. Regardless, everyone was excited to be on the mountain and ready to begin the day's climb.

After breakfast, we donned our packs and gathered our gear for the second day of the climb and made our way to the northern edge of camp where we paused briefly to survey what lay ahead of us for the day. To the northeast, Kibo was unmistakable. Steven pointed to the northwest toward the Shira Plateau, indicating the direction of our Day 2 destination, unseen from our current vantage point.

The terrain immediately before us appeared similar to the smooth topped mountains of Appalachia in Tennessee and North Carolina near where I was born and grew up, but with completely different vegetation. Gone were the tall, dense trees of the rainforest, and in their place were tall, skinny heather. I was amazed by how different the landscape was from the southern to the northern boundaries of Machame Camp, which didn't seem large at all.

On this day, we would hike approximately 3.1 miles, the same distance as a 5K race. Rather than the 30-35 minutes typically required to run 5K, it would take several hours to cover the distance. Beginning at an elevation of approximately 9,900 feet, we would hike/climb roughly 2,700 feet upward to Shira Camp, which sits at 12,595 feet above sea level. Steep climbs before the midway break and undulating hills as we neared the Shira plateau awaited us (Stedman, 2010, p. 268). Since the group had some time to acclimatize over the previous twenty-four hours, I hoped we could pick up the pace from that of the day before, which had seemed excruciatingly slow at times.

After months of researching the Machame Route and how the daily climbs would be broken up, I anticipated Day 2 would be the most similar to a mountain hike in the States. The terrain and elevation were similar to several places I had hiked and trained in Colorado during the several months preceding the climb, and the weather should be sunny and semi-arid as compared to the humidity of the rain forest during the previous day. For me, Day 2 was more about people. My goal was to enjoy the hike while getting to know my teammates better and listen to their stories during the day. We would also have more opportunities to interact with our Tanzanian counterparts, one of whom I would soon call my friend.

As the initial climb was steep, it didn't take long to reach a point where I could look back and see from where we had come. Gone from view was most of the rainforest and all of the vast African plains. The Machame Camp appeared to be situated on a coastline bordering a vast sea of clouds extending as far as I could see to the south. It was the first time we could look back and see the result of our effort on Day 1. The slow, steady plodding through the rainforest had felt like walking on an inclined treadmill all day, but we had made serious progress. For most of the remainder of Day 2, we would be able to stop briefly to survey how far we had progressed and be rewarded with spectacular views.

This morning was different from the first in regard to actually seeing the level of support required for our trek up the mountain. During the previous day while our group was going through the registration process and waiting for the notification to begin the climb, several of the assistant guides, porters, and cooks had gone on before us, unseen until we reached the Machame Camp. Today, they were scattered. I noticed some of the porters started carrying our duffel bags before we began our climb, but the majority stayed to help break camp before proceeding up the trail.

Periodically throughout the morning, a porter or cook would catch up to the group, greet us in Swahili with *jambo* (hello) and, as we moved aside to let them pass, *asante* (thank you) or *asante sana* (thank you very much). The interactions allowed the members of the group to put the few bits of Swahili we had learned leading up the climb to use when we replied with *jambo* or *habari* (how are you?). We heard *pole pole* (slowly, slowly) often. A few of the Tanzanians would say *Hakuna matata* (no worries), which we easily recognized, as they passed. *Hakuna matata*, made popular by its use in *The Lion King* movie, is not a common term used in Tanzania. It is used primarily by those who work in the Tanzanian tourist industry.

It's easy to be impressed with the young Tanzanian men who work on Kilimanjaro. The thin, fit men swiftly carried baggage nearly a third of their body weight up the mountain. Their disposition was one that stated confidence and strength. That which seemed like an extraordinary burden to me was just a normal day's work for them. They were warm and friendly in their interactions with us, and extremely easy to like. They had a genuine curiosity about us as people and the culture of America, but also expressed great love for Tanzania and enjoyed sharing their land and culture with us in return.

One thing in particular struck me as I watched them move with ease up the mountain: The climbers in our group had spent several hundred dollars each on boots, clothing, and gear to make the trek up Kilimanjaro, yet the Tanzanian porters were making the same journey carrying heavier loads while wearing worn out sneakers or boots with little tread remaining, jeans, and old cotton shirts. The guides fared only slightly better.

Most of them seemed to enjoy what they were doing and had cheerful demeanors and positive attitudes. A few young, first time porters were nearly as unsure of where they were going as the climbers, and the weight of their loads was definitely a new experience. My respect for the Tanzanians grew with each passing moment on the trail, and I silently made a vow to not complain about anything while on the mountain.

Although separated by only a few yards, we were spread out into smaller groups of three or four on the narrow, steep trail. I spent the first hour or so of the climb with Tyler, Dan, and Brad near the back of the pack. The four of us had bonded quickly at the hotel and during the first day. We told jokes and stories and laughed like we had known each other for years. Will spent a few minutes with us before moving on to give individual attention to other members of the group.

As the climb became steeper and the elevation rose quickly, we stopped frequently for short breaks. The sun became a factor early on, unlike the first day of the climb, as we were out in the open. Spots offering a small area of shade became pit stops on the trek. The open terrain also affected bathroom breaks, especially for the women. It had been relatively easy to find a well hidden spot to heed the call of nature in the dense rain forest, but privacy on this part of the mountain was at a premium. A waist-high rock a few yards off the trail became a luxury port-a-potty for the women of the group, while the men would just walk off the trail and face away from the group to take care of their business. Those who were bashful about taking care of the necessary the day prior were becoming like old pros at it on Day 2.

During the pit stops and rest breaks we were able to take the time to catch glimpses of the peak and views of the area we had already covered. I was awestruck by the sheer size of the mountain. Everything I could see in any direction was part of Mt. Kilimanjaro. I had time during the breaks to reflect on not just the previous seven months of my Kilimanjaro journey, but on all that had transpired over the past decade eventually leading to where I stood on this stretch of the Machame Route.

Just as the trail wound its way up from the flat land below through the rain forest, the heather zone where our group was now passing, and the moorland, alpine desert, and glacial zones that lay before us on the trek to Uhuru Peak, the road I had traveled had passed through several phases and taken many twists and turns. The possibility of making a journey such as this had been impossible for so many years, yet I was here looking out across a part of the earth that so few have seen in person.

I'm amazed by a God who could create such a giant, beautiful, singular mountain in the middle of the East African plains. Even more amazing is a God who would care enough about a single broken man, one of more than seven billion inhabitants of earth, to pick him up off of the scrap heap, rebuild his body and life and give him the crazy and awesome task of climbing the tallest freestanding mountain on the globe. For what purpose, I did not know, but I trust Him to do amazing things with what seems impossible or crazy to most.

20

BALANCE

I have never let my schooling interfere with my education.

MARK TWAIN

The two months between mid-October and mid-December 2010 were a roller coaster of events, emotions, and life changes. The 2/9 blanket project had given me the opportunity to come out of my isolation to do something for others. I learned something about myself and the compassion and willingness of others to rise to the occasion. I had an idea born out of love for my son and extended it to his Marine brothers, made a plan and enlisted the help of others, then made some good things happen.

Max was progressing through the steps to become a Marine, and would soon reach the point of signing enlistment documents and swearing the same oath his older brother had sworn to uphold. Liv and I were coming to terms with our reservations, and were even becoming excited for him and his sense of adult-like direction.

The incredible changes to my body and overall health were becoming more evident as time progressed. The momentum of the long, downward spiral had been brought to a halt and was slowly turning around in the opposite direction. The difficult moments of despair thinking about Eli were becoming easier to navigate as I learned to rely more on faith and focusing on God for reassurance and direction.

By mid-December, I was closer than ever before to the goal of finally standing on Ten Mile Rock, having reached the point of being able to walk eight miles in one day. The cane and leg brace were now merely dust magnets in the entry hall closet. In less than three months, my walk seemed normal for much of the day, only regressing slightly as the day progressed and the fatigue arrived later each evening. Somewhat surprisingly, I was becoming less symptomatic overall.

It seemed odd to be experiencing such a rebirth in my own life while Eli's was in peril every moment of the day, but I had no doubt the two were connected. We were both striving to make it through to the other side. I also believe hope is contagious. From the most recent communication with him, Eli sounded cautiously optimistic as the frequency of firefights while on patrol and attacks instigated by the Taliban had decreased significantly with the onset of cold weather, and were expected to decrease further during the coldest winter months.

The 2/9 Marines had wreaked havoc on the Taliban in Marjah district. As their casualties mounted, the Taliban spent longer periods of time licking their wounds before attempting to attack the Marines again. For the first time in many months, Eli allowed himself the luxury of talking about what he wanted to do if he made it home. He spoke of what he'd like to do during his post-deployment leave, especially the foods he would eat.

He and his fellow Marines would torture each other as they drifted off whenever the opportunity for sleep came, describing in great detail their favorite meals made by family members and restaurants. Eli called it gastrosadomasochism: tempting each other with unattainable foods until it drove someone crazy. Knowing his sense of humor and his oratory skills, I'm sure he won his fair share of the gastrosadomasochism games.

The subject of food occupied my thoughts, too. The post-surgery progression from liquids, to soft, puréed food, to solid foods was complete. I knew I couldn't return to the careless, unhealthy eating habits that had been the result of compulsive behaviors caused by some of the Parkinson's medications, compounded by mental fatigue and weakness. I also wanted to eliminate as many unnecessary chemicals as possible from entering my body, including those in processed foods.

During the weeks I was on a limited diet, I researched various nutrition options including those offered by the nutritionist who worked with the bariatric doctor who performed my surgery. I wanted something that was both radical but not a passing fad. I've found the "quick and easy" fix usually isn't the best option. Things that require effort and hard work are.

After eight weeks of eating simply, the desire for unhealthy foods had been broken. I no longer wanted foods rich in sugar and salt and other additives that make our bodies crave empty calories. I wanted food that was simple, fresh, and nutrient dense. The hook that reeled me in was a phrase that seemed to come up often: Eat like your grandparents did.

My grandparents weren't the healthiest people I've ever known, but I got the point. In early twentieth century America, the era in which my grandparents were born and came of age, most people either farmed, grew vegetables and fruits in their gardens, or shopped at local farmers' markets, grocers, and butcher shops. They gathered fresh foods and cooked what they needed for the meals that day. It's not a coincidence that the rise in obesity rates and obesity-related health issues over the last half century has coincided with the rise of the fast food industry and the advent of large grocery chains with pre-packaged foods transported from faraway locations.

The amount of information available regarding food and nutritional choices is overwhelming and confusing, and is the source of much consternation for people seeking to make life changes that result in weight loss and healthier living. We humans have a tendency to overcomplicate things, and I am just as guilty as the next person. However, the cognitive changes brought about by the progression of the Parkinson's over the years have forced me to change how I approach problem solving. When confused or overwhelmed by complexity, I have no choice but to stop and employ the KISS principle: Keep It Simple, Stupid.

For me this meant two things: Eat whole, fresh foods in their natural state, and eat those foods in quantities and combinations that fuel the level of activity over the course of a given day. By mid-December, I had lost sixty-five pounds, far exceeding the hopes and estimates of my physicians. I wasn't done though. I sought to look in the mirror for the first time in years and see the person I was before Parkinson's, at least on the outside.

I began experiencing an unexpected reaction to the exercise and nutritional changes. As the Parkinson's symptoms began to subside with the increase in physical activity, change in diet, and drop in weight and body mass, the side effects of the medications worsened. In essence, as my weight dropped precipitously, it had the effect of a sudden increase in the dosage of medications. Working with Dr. Nicholas, we began decreasing the dosage of each Parkinson's medication and the side effects subsided quickly.

Trial and error with medications, the most common treatment option used by physicians who treat Parkinson's, had caused many ups and downs over the first eight years of my experience with the disease. The first significant shift in the battle had come only when I bought into taking a more holistic approach. From my experience, the improvement in symptom management and quality of life had come only after the addition of exercise, nutrition, and most importantly, a positive attitude, to the mix. Each treatment element plays an integral role in not only managing, but also gaining the upper hand on Parkinson's. The key is balance.

Treatment options other than medication are often left to the person with Parkinson's to discover. Physicians will offer advice regarding exercise, proper nutrition, and managing stress, but it is up to the individual to take action. I was in the midst of discovering that I wasn't powerless after all against the monster that had tormented me for so long. Perhaps it took longer for me than others fighting the battle to discover the tools at my disposal. Unfortunately, many people with Parkinson's never do.

21

ECHO TO SANGIN (HELL, PART 2)

Weird things happen suddenly,
and your life can go all to pieces.

HUNTER S. THOMPSON

The positive momentum hit a major road block just after Christmas with a late night phone call from Sam. When I answered his call, he blurted out, "They're sending Echo to Sangin!"

My heart jumped then immediately sank as I struggled to process the words. My mind raced ahead to complete his sentence before he finished it, and hoped he was saying Echo was being sent to Camp Leatherneck, the largest Marine Corps base in Afghanistan and the last waypoint before leaving the country. But as the word Sangin reached my brain, hope was crushed and bewilderment took its place.

Sam had an uncanny ability to discern what our sons faced based on bits and pieces of information he gathered and studied during the many sleepless nights fighting his version of the monster we both faced. God, how I hoped he was wrong.

The Sangin district of Helmand Province is located approximately seventy miles northeast of Marjah in the Helmand River valley. It is an infamous Taliban stronghold, known as one of the deadliest locations in Afghanistan. For years, the Taliban had been fighting with concentrated effort to protect one of the central locations for the opium trade in the southern part of the country.

Earlier in 2010, the Taliban had been overwhelmed by the Marines coming to the aid of British forces and who had eventually taken over operations in the area, but had pushed back with fervor. The 3d Battalion, 5th Marines, out of Camp Pendleton, California, had been deployed in Sangin since October and had suffered significant casualties in the first three months of their time there. If a Marine wanted to see intense combat, he got his wish once on the ground in Sangin.

"What are you talking about, Sam?" I asked with both astonishment and a sense of urgency.

"Have you heard from Eli?" he replied with a rapid-fire question of his own.

"Today? No. We spoke last week, and he as much as said they had run the Taliban out of Marjah and thought they might be able to coast through their remaining time there with the onset of winter." I assured him, and asked again, "What are you talking about?"

He stated grimly, "Well, it's going to get really messy, my friend."

Sam went on to explain that during his conversation with his son earlier in the day, Kyle had told him that he would be out of touch for a few weeks because he would be helping some friends take care of some business. His tone and his vague, cryptic words had told Sam all he needed to know.

I could picture Kyle on the other end of the line in Afghanistan making facial expressions like De Niro in one of his gangster or mob type movie roles. He was a jokester even when serious, but his dad knew how to read him. Just the thought of Kyle caused a suppressed chuckle, even in the midst of the startling turn of events Sam had just shared with me.

I had met Kyle when I dropped Eli off at Thompson-Boling Arena on the campus of the University of Tennessee in Knoxville to hitch a ride with him back to Camp Lejeune in his beat up Tahoe before their leave ended. His sense of humor was evident from the first moment we met, and I knew my son had bonded with him as if blood kin. They would have each other's backs when things got tough.

I didn't want to believe Sam, and hoped for once his ability to see the way things could play out was wrong. While still on the phone, we began scouring the private Facebook Marine family group postings for any information that could confirm or allay our concerns. We knew something was brewing by the sheer number of people active in the group during the late night hours.

Although monitored by Marine parents who took OPSEC seriously, there was a subtle language used between the parents and families of the warfighters that relayed information between the lines of text. What appeared to be meaningless banter among members of the group was actually pieces of the puzzle that allowed us to understand without jeopardizing OPSEC.

Exhausted and anxious, Sam and I decided to end our late night conversation. I hoped he was mistaken, but we both believed he wasn't. We agreed to let the other know as soon as we heard some news, regardless of the time of day or night. Just as I thought we had passed through the toughest part of the storm and would soon see our sons again, the winds suddenly shifted and increased in ferocity and the storm clouds on the near horizon were terribly dark indeed.

I knew this was one burden I would carry alone for as I long as I could bear it. Liv had been much happier in the last few weeks since she had picked up on Eli's lighter tone and mood, and like him, had begun talking about the things we would do together as a family after homecoming.

A couple of excruciatingly slow days passed before Eli called. When Liv handed the phone to me, the happy expression on her face was like a punch to my gut because I didn't want to take her happiness from her with the news I had been withholding. I took the phone and walked outside to talk. It was something Liv was accustomed to seeing me do while on the phone with Eli, so it didn't seem out of the ordinary to her.

I hoped he would let me know that something had changed, but he didn't. He carried on as though he was enjoying the break from action in Marjah. When I asked if he had changed locations, he became as cautious as if he was walking through an IED-laden field. We both understood the rules of engagement. OPSEC is critical when troops are on the move. The rest of the conversation consisted of vague questions and reluctant non-answers, but I understood. I told him I loved him, hoping it wasn't the last time I would get to do so.

"I love you, too, old man," he replied using his favorite term of affection for me. "Keep up the good work on your end, hug mom for me, and tell Max to get his stuff straight and to be sure it's what he wants before he signs those papers and swears the oath. I gotta go. Not sure when I'll be able to call. Hang in there," his voice trailing off as the call ended. My son sounded as if he was saying his last goodbye, just in case.

Before I went inside, I dialed Sam's number. "I spoke to Eli. It's confirmed," was all I could manage to say before ending the call.

22

25,000 STEPS

If you can't fly then run,
if you can't run then walk,
if you can't walk then crawl,
but whatever you do
you have to keep moving forward.

MARTIN LUTHER KING, JR.

On the morning of January 4, 2011, Max received his wake up call at 4:45 a.m. in his hotel room in Montgomery, Alabama. Soon thereafter, he was taken to the MEPS facility nearby to begin a long day of questions and medical examinations that would determine whether he would indeed become a United States Marine. Our family was well-acquainted with MEPS, or a Military Entrance Processing Station. He had already taken the ASVAB (Armed Services Vocational Aptitude Battery) at the Birmingham recruiting station and passed with high scores. He had also completed and submitted the medical prescreening documents. No surprises were expected to arise at MEPS.

Barring an unexpected disqualification before leaving the facility, Max would swear his Oath of Enlistment, sign his enlistment contract, and officially enter the Delayed Entry Program just as his older brother had done at the same location four and a half years earlier. He, too, was destined to be an Infantry grunt.

I rose early that morning as well. The day felt surreal as I thought about what Max would be doing that day. My youngest child would soon leave home. I had been a parent for half my life, and I was struggling with the reality that soon neither of my children would be part of my everyday, and that I couldn't see their faces or reach out to hug them if I wanted. I was still coming to grips with the new reality that Eli had fulfilled his mission in Marjah only to be sent to one of the most violent places in Afghanistan. Two Echo Company Marines had been KIA in Sangin in their first week there, bringing the total number of 2/9 casualties to fourteen.

After Liv left for work, I readied for what else this day would bring. I knew this would be the day I would make the attempt to stand on Ten Mile Rock. The day had too much significance for me to fail. Just after sunrise, I put on my cold gear and drove the short distance to the trailhead. For the next three-plus hours I would walk. Just three months prior I had made my first lap around the lake trail taking slow, painful steps on legs underdeveloped from disease and lack of use. There was a lot more of me then, too. Since that first lap, I had lost nearly eighty pounds, and the person I saw in the mirror looked more and more like someone I knew long ago.

There were so many thoughts swirling around in my mind when I started that I don't remember beginning the walk. It doesn't matter though, because it was a continuation of the longer journey, each step taking me closer to where I was supposed to be. I had been at it long enough that it no longer felt like something I would do *someday* or something that seemed as impossible as it had on that first day. I felt further from the starting point than from my destination. No longer did I need to concentrate on every step I took. My legs and my body had become accustomed to moving in sync again, as if detours and new pathways had formed in my brain to take the signals from origination to destination.

As I circled the lake, my thoughts drifted back and forth from Max and what he was doing, to Eli in the fight of his life on the other side of the world. I thought about Sam who was thinking the same thoughts about his son, and the hundreds of other parents, spouses, and children of not only the Marines of the 2/9, but all those who had a loved one serving in a war zone. I thought about the wounded and the fallen. Specifically, I mourned the fourteen vibrant young men who had paid the ultimate price while serving our country, and I grieved for their families. I tried to recite each of their names as I saw their faces in my mind. I knew their faces, the brothers of my son. I did not know it that day, but the list of the fallen was not yet complete.

I couldn't escape the question: Would I join those Gold Star families so close to the end of the deployment? When the thought invaded my mind, it nearly brought me to my knees as involuntarily as if someone swept my legs from under me. I had to pause each time it came, and I cried out, "Please, God, please, spare my son. I will be there to help him if he comes home wounded. I will love him, no matter what. Please, Lord, let me see my son again!" And each time, I would begin moving forward again, obeying the simple command and direction God had given me through the simple, yet profound story about the man who pushed the rock.

As the GPS tracking app on my phone showed that I was nearing eight miles, my previous longest distance walked, my legs were tired and movement was slowly regressing. But I couldn't stop before reaching the goal. I thought about my sons again, and reached deep down into the well of love that has grown since the days they were born, and found the fire I needed to keep going.

The last few laps burned and exhaustion was close, but when I passed the rock for the last time, I knew the next time I was that close to it I would finally stand on it. I completed the thirteenth lap at the trailhead and reversed course back toward the rock. In the future when approaching a mountain summit, I would always remember the feeling of hard fought accomplishment as I approached the rock. To the rest of the world, it was just a big rock by a neighborhood lake, but to me it was the first summit. My first summit. My rock.

As I stepped up onto the rock for the first time, I didn't feel the sweat quickly turning ice cold underneath my clothes, or my nose running and freezing on my mustache, or my cold toes and feet. I felt the warmth of reaching a peak in life, even in the midst of the turmoil both inside me and in the world over which I had no control. I felt proud of my sons and their desire to serve our country. They had inspired me to become a better man.

I took off my gloves and let my hands discover the contours and the textures of the rock I had sought for months. I climbed a few mores steps and stood on the highest point and looked at the lake and trail, the place where I felt most at home for much of the previous three months, from a new perspective.

I scanned the heavens hoping for some divine revelation. But the only thought that came to mind was to keep moving. Although I had reached a significant milestone in my recovery, I had not yet arrived at my destination. I savored the accomplishment for several minutes, stepped off the rock then moved forward, the only direction I could go.

23

KILIMANJARO: DAY 2 - SHIRA CAMP

25 AUG 2012

The rolling hills and steep, rocky switchbacks of the trail we encountered after turning in a northwesterly direction away from Kibo required focus to prevent falls and twisted ankles or knees. As the group neared the tops of ridgelines, we were able to see porters and members of other groups ahead of us on the trail, which gave us an idea of where we were heading. The trail snaked up and down the hills ahead of us.

Unintentionally, I found myself among four wonderful women on the hike after taking a break for snacks to get us through until we reached camp and could have a late lunch. Ava and Lizzie were college roommate nearly a decade earlier, and had remained friends since, even though Lizzie lived in New York City and Ava had moved upstate for her career. They had traveled together often over the years, but had a tough time recently lining up their schedules for an adventure. When the opportunity to climb Kilimanjaro came about, they made their schedules work to be able to do so. Both seemed genuinely happy with their lives. They asked questions about my family and how I came to be on the climb, and I shared some of the long road it had taken to reach the point where we were at the moment.

Kate and Bella worked together at a well-known cancer treatment center in New York City. Kate was still trying to put her arms around the fact that she was actually climbing Kilimanjaro. She wasn't an avid hiker and had never thought about climbing the mountain until Bella proposed the idea to her coworkers while seeking a partner for the climb. She admitted that it was out of character for her to be impulsive, but something about the trip struck a chord within her and she agreed to take on the challenge.

Bella was one of the most adventurous members of the group. Earlier in the year, she had traveled to South America to hike the Inca Trail to Machu Picchu, the fifteenth century Inca site, in the Cusco Region of Peru. Her career afforded her the resources to travel, and she took full advantage of her opportunities. She and her sister had been raised by their father to love outdoors activities and seek out rare experiences. Her life was full with work, travel, and continuing her education. I was impressed by her wit, attitude, previous experiences, and outlook, especially for someone in her twenties.

The afternoon sun was relentless as we continued the climb. When we reached a large cliff overhang resembling an open cave, we stopped for a break. The heat, combined with the elevation gain, necessitated longer breaks. The cliff overhang offered the most shade we had seen up until this point. It was an opportunity to cool off, apply some sunscreen, and ensure adequate hydration. The view of the peak was excellent from this vantage point, and everyone broke out his or her camera to snap photos. A large boulder adjacent to the cliff overhang was a perfect spot to pose, and several of the women of the group gathered together on the boulder to get a group shot. They stood like conquerors, each pointing at Kilimanjaro's peak.

Not long after resuming the climb, one of the young porters had a mishap and fell, injuring him slightly. The strap on his overstuffed backpack broke, and the shifting of the weight of the duffel he carried on top of his backpack brought him crashing to the ground. He seemed more embarrassed than hurt. Dan, Brad, and I stopped to see if we could help as the remainder of the group continued slowly upward.

The knife and small spool of 550 paracord that I carried everywhere with me for such situations was put to use. It was also the first opportunity for substantial interaction with an assistant guide named Dismass, who assisted the porter with the repair. Lean and muscular in his late thirties, he appeared much younger physically, but much older because of his calming and knowledgeable presence. He used the knife and paracord to quickly repair the backpack and help the young man on his way. Once again, I was reminded of the disparity in equipment between the American climbers and the Tanzanian crew. I wanted to do something about it, but wasn't sure what that might be.

Dismass stayed at the rear with Dan, Brad, and me until we reached the Shira Plateau and caught up with the rest of the group. It gave us the opportunity to ask questions about the lives of those who work on Kilimanjaro. Dismass shared about his family and how long he had worked the mountain. He started out as a porter in his teens and had worked his way through a career progression to assistant guide. He had summited Kilimanjaro over one-hundred times, and hoped to become a lead guide soon. Working on Kilimanjaro was among the most sought after occupations in Tanzania. Few ever left a career working on the mountain for something else with the exception of an injury that prevented one from fulfilling his duties.

Once we reached the Shira Plateau, the terrain leveled considerably, and we had beautiful views of Johnsell Point and Klute Peak, the highest points on the Shira Ridge, and of Mt. Meru farther in the distance. Now above 12,000 feet, the wind picked up and the temperature dropped considerably. Shira Camp became visible after a short slope. It is a large encampment on a relatively flat spot of ground void of vegetation other than a few small Acacia trees. A multi-colored array of tents was spread in clusters out across the clearing.

It was mid-afternoon when we arrived at camp, much earlier in the day than we had reached camp on Day 1. When we chose our tents, I was able to score one of the single occupancy ones. The lack of restful sleep the night prior combined with the travel and physical exertion of the past few days had brought me closer to the monster than I had been in quite some time. I needed some solid rest if I hoped to reach the summit.

After the late lunch, we were given a few hours to rest before going out for a two-hour acclimatization hike prior to the evening meal. The wind was relentless, and inside the tent the flapping of the tent fabric was deafening. It didn't matter though. I set my alarm for the designated time and was lights out in an instant.

When the rest break in our tents ended, we gathered for the acclimatization hike. In just a few hours, the wind had picked up even more speed, which made it feel much colder. Most members of the group took a few moments to add another layer of cold gear before making the hike. The purpose of the hike was simple. Now that we were above 10,000 feet, we would follow the well-known practice of "climb-high, sleep-low." Sleeping at a lower elevation than climbed in a given day would help to avoid altitude sickness.

To aid in the acclimatization process, some climbers take the prescription medication Diamox. Several members of the group who were coming from sea level or low elevations had chosen to begin taking the drug as a preventative measure before starting the climb. The travel physician I had visited to receive the necessary and recommended vaccinations had prescribed it for me, and suggested that I take it a few times before traveling to Tanzania, which I had done several weeks prior. Other than mildly numb lips, I had felt no side effects from taking the trial dose of the drug.

I had been to elevations above 14,000 feet with no problems, but this night would be the decision point to begin using the Diamox. It needed to be in my system for at least forty-eight hours prior to reaching and staying above elevations I had not previously climbed. While training on the Colorado mountains, I had learned from experienced climbers and hikers that using ibuprofen was effective for warding off the minor symptoms of altitude sickness. I had used the ibuprofen several times during training, and I preferred to stick to what I knew worked for me.

Heading east, we followed the path we would take on Day 3. The massive peak was directly in front of us as we made our way slowly upward while getting closer to the alpine desert. We stopped after approximately fifty minutes, having gained close to 1,000 feet in elevation. Each of us found a spot to sit and rest while quietly looking at Kilimanjaro's peak. I was awestruck by its massive size and beauty. The sky was a deep blue, and clouds swirled around the peak obstructing the view of the summit. We posed for group photos before beginning the descent back to camp. First, the entire group of sixteen posed together then the ten Team Fox members posed with a large Team Fox banner to document this portion of the climb for the Foundation.

At more than 12,000 feet, there are no bad views on Kilimanjaro. Just as we had been mesmerized by the peak on the ascent portion of the acclimatization hike, the views of Shira Camp, Johnsell Point and Klute Peak beyond it, and Mt. Meru on the horizon at sunset on the descent into camp were spectacular. It was the kind of place people seek out as a destination spot in the United States.

The evening meal was almost ready when we returned to camp. We had just enough time to stow our packs and clean up before gathering in the meal tent. As the temperature dropped below freezing outside the tent, it was only slightly warmer inside. The only light was from candles and headlamps. The meal was a feast of wedge-cut potatoes, green beans and carrots, cucumbers and tomatoes, and select portions of tender meat. We shared stories about the day's hike, and shared the bad and good things that stood out for each of us that day. We ate like kings and stuffed ourselves. We would have eaten even more had we known it would be the best meal we would have on the mountain.

Later, while bundled in my sleeping bag I held the prescription bottle in my hand. By the light of my headlamp, I read every word on the label. Taking the drug could make the difference between making it to the summit or not. It should have been an easy decision, but it wasn't. My struggle with Parkinson's medications during the past decade made the decision difficult. Should I take the drug and increase my chances of summiting, or refuse to take it and risk everything I had worked so hard to achieve and possibly fail? Finally, I stuffed the unopened pill bottle down into the depths of my duffel bag and extinguished my headlamp. Succeed or fail, I needed to do this on my own.

24

THE GREEN HATS OF MARJAH

Marines don't know how to spell the word defeat.

GENERAL JAMES N. MATTIS, USMC (RET.)

On the far side of the world, the men repeated a ritual they had executed more than a thousand times during the previous six and a half months. Their training and experience allowed them to move with machine-like efficiency as they prepared to once again step outside the wire into one of the most dangerous places on earth. Each of the young yet old men, the Green Hats of Marjah, were focused on the task before them, checking and double-checking their weapons and gear as their breath and cigarette smoke formed a cloud that hovered over them on the cold January day in southern Afghanistan.

Although they tried to bury the thought deep inside, they knew this patrol was different. If they could just make it through to the other side ... *No!*, they couldn't allow the thought to invade their minds. It would only remind them of the total exhaustion their bodies knew but their minds fought to convince them of otherwise. They couldn't—*no, they wouldn't!*—allow the almost attainable yet still forbidden thoughts of freedom and the completion of their months-long mission to cloud their judgment and interfere with their objective. It could cost them their lives if they did.

Weeks earlier, the men of Echo Company, 2d Battalion, 9th Marines, had come approximately one-hundred kilometers north to Sangin with a reputation that preceded them among the Taliban fighters. The story of how they received their unofficial moniker would one day become part of Marine Corps lore.

Desert digi-cammies were the norm, but early in the deployment this company of Marines had taken the initiative to turn their helmet covers to the green side for better concealment as they patrolled the farmland and the vast network of old irrigation canals in the Marjah district. Shrouded by the greenery that grew near the man-made sources of water, the canals were the primary routes the Taliban used for transporting opium throughout the moderately flat parts of the country.

Not long after beginning operations in Sangin, a letter from one Taliban commander to another in the area was found near a patrol base, warning them to beware the American Marines with the green covers on their helmets. The document warned that the "green hats" were dangerous and were to be avoided if possible, as they fought ferociously and had caused many Taliban casualties in Marjah.

These brothers from different mothers and locations around the United States had converged on the desolate, rocky terrain of an ages-old, war-torn, godforsaken country and had laid waste to the enemy. Today there were no jokes or casual conversation among a small contingent of Echo Marines as they readied themselves for what was to come. The body heat emanating from their grimy, sweat covered bodies churned from beneath their helmets, their collars, and the ends of their sleeves as it mixed with the sub-freezing air, symbolic of the controlled rage each man felt after the recent loss of three Echo Marines. As a result of operations security, the intentional lack of communication, and the time difference between the United States and Afghanistan, none of the family members of the Green Hats knew that as they slept, their sons or brothers or husbands downrange were stepping outside the wire to take it to the enemy one last time before coming home.

Nearly two weeks had passed since we had spoken to our son. He had called to let us know he was okay for the moment, but deeply saddened by the loss of three Marines during their first week in Sangin. The last of which, and the fifteenth KIA since the deployment began, was a close friend with whom he had spent a lot of time both on and off duty. The call was difficult and brief and we hadn't heard his voice since.

The brief emotional high I felt when I finally reached the Ten Mile Rock milestone was followed by one of the most difficult periods of my life. Every day leading up to the end of Eli's deployment seemed to pass more slowly than the one before, and the weight of the cumulative tension and anxiety was crushing our family.

The mood inside our home felt like three members of the famous Flying Wallendas walking a single tightrope at the same time over the world's deepest crevasse. The tension was palpable as we tried to coordinate our movements as to not upset the delicate balance of the other two on the tightrope. We knew there were hundreds of other families across the country walking tightropes similar to ours, all hoping to make it to the end without hearing the news that would bring them crashing down.

We didn't choose to be on the high-wire, yet here we were. Retreat wasn't possible. Our only hope to make it was to continue inching forward, the end within sight yet so far away. There were countless moments when we tried not to freeze from the fear, desperately wanting to just close our eyes and forget about the crevasse beneath us. In those moments, I learned just how thin the line is between sanity and madness.

25

KILIMANJARO: DAY 3 - LAVA TOWER

26 AUG 2012

The loud hum of the tent material vibrating with the relentless wind the night before made it easy to shift my brain into neutral. I reached the terminal velocity of the fall into deep sleep in mere seconds. The same wind bearing down on Shira Camp that aided my slumber a few hours before was also responsible for waking me.

After years or months or perhaps only weeks of holding fast against the forces of nature, several nails holding a tin roofing panel in place on a lonely little shack at the edge of the camp finally gave way, allowing the metal to beat loudly against wood and itself to create an eclectic drumming sound. Unable to ignore the odd, irritating percussion, my unconscious mind surrendered to the start of the day.

Awake at just before four in the morning with little hope of falling asleep again, I decided to catch up on journaling. As I chronicled the events of the day prior by the light of my headlamp, I savored my current situation. I was alone in this small tent on the side of a giant mountain in Africa. The fabric of the tent, the sleeping bag, and the clothes on my back were my only barriers against the elements.

Hours away from the creature comforts of civilization, I felt more free than I had during those years of my life spent at the mercy of modern medicine. The prison my body had become—and dependence on others for some of the basic needs of life—seemed like a fading nightmare here in this remote and incredibly beautiful place reachable only by foot. Although the number of miles traveled on my own legs to reach this spot on the mountain was easily quantifiable, the struggle to overcome the years of being less than wasn't as easily measured.

When the glow of first light began turning the dark fabric surrounding me to a lighter shade, I could no longer stay within the confines of the tent. Other than the porters and cooks stirring to life, I was the first of our group to enter the elements. The early morning was cold and cloudy and although the wind was still formidable, it had lost some of its ferocity. I took advantage of being first to use the bathroom tent then ventured beyond the camp boundary. I wanted a few solitary moments to myself out in the open before beginning the day's climb. I took the path from the day before on the acclimatization hike, the same one we would soon take as a group. I didn't have to go far for it to feel like I was all alone on the mountain.

I found a suitable rock and sat to observe the peak. I was in an area where I could see beyond the scrub to the transition to alpine desert. Photos of the peak cannot capture what is seen with the naked eye. The mountain is alive. The static, dull gray clouds directly overhead gave way to bright white ones in the distance that swirled with beautifully choreographed movement up, around, and down the peak, resulting in the dance between light and darkness on the surfaces of the peak and slopes. Virtually untouched by man, God is ever present in His majesty in the mountains. Awestruck by what I what I saw and felt surrounding me, I was humbled by my place in the world.

In the months leading up to the climb, there had been conversations with some who had the misconception that climbing Kilimanjaro is relatively easy. "Isn't it just a long walk uphill?" they asked. There had been nothing easy about the preparation for or the climb so far, and the ground to be covered for the remainder of the climb would only get tougher. If I had any doubts about just how difficult it would be to reach the summit, they were put to rest during the few moments of solitude spent studying the peak. The final ascent would be one of the hardest physical challenges I would ever undertake. The terrain is difficult, but when combined with the thin air, it is beyond treacherous. Only the uneducated could think reaching the peak is easy.

Several minutes later, I made my way back to camp for breakfast. By the time I reached the edge of camp, I saw most of my teammates outside their tents in various stages of final preparations for the day's trek. One in particular caught my attention. Bella moved slowly away from the tent she shared with Kate, and emptied multiple bladder-like containers of liquid. It seemed odd considering the effort required to get our drinking water. We used every last drop. Water was gathered by porters from designated sources then boiled to sterilize it before distribution to climbers and support personnel. But it wasn't water in the containers Bella was emptying.

I didn't have to wonder about her actions for long. At break-fast it was evident to all that Bella was ill. She had been awake for much of the night, the nausea overwhelming her several times. Afterward when we gathered to begin the climb, Bella indicated that although she didn't feel her best she had no other apparent symptoms of altitude sickness and was deter-mined to continue the climb. She was the first to show the signs and effects of climbing at high altitude.

Ten kilometers stood between our group and Barranco Camp, our destination for the day. Sitting at the base of the Barranco Wall, the primary challenge awaiting us tomorrow, Barranco Camp is less than five hundred feet higher in eleva-tion than our current location at Shira Camp. However, our path would first lead us to the Lava Tower, higher in elevation than all of the mountains in the lower forty-eight states, be-fore descending to camp. Climb high, sleep low. After ascend-ing several thousand feet from the Machame Gate over the first two days of the climb, the gradual rise and fall in eleva-tion of the Day 3 trek is necessary for acclimatization before continuing up the mountain.

We left camp and began moving east through and eventu-ally away from the Shira Plateau. The first forty-five minutes of the hike covered the same ground as the day before, and we stopped for a break at the same location where we had turned around previously. Breaks are always welcome, but the primary purpose of this one was to allow Will and Steven to check on Bella. Although the nausea she felt during the night was still present to some degree, she didn't appear to show other, troublesome signs of altitude sickness. She wanted to continue the climb.

When we moved beyond the plateau into the Alpine desert zone, we entered familiar ground for me. In Colorado, where I had trained during the spring and summer, the tree line marks the point in a climb when it becomes much more difficult. Above tree line, typically around 11,500 feet, movement becomes more difficult with increasing elevation. Everything slows down, and breaks are needed more often to offset fatigue. An inexperienced climber will continue moving up a mountain trail until near exhaustion forces them to take a break, and it becomes increasingly difficult to continue after resting. A surprise headache will often come with the swiftness of a blow to the head. Just as an experienced runner can foretell how his body will react at a specific mile point in a long-distance race, I knew how my body would react at altitude and how I would need to proceed over the remaining distance to be covered. My time in the Rockies had taught me the hard way, and a better way to move up a mountain.

Many trailheads in the Rockies sit at elevations between 8,000-10,000 feet, which aren't much higher than that of my home. When I first started climbing at altitude, I charged up a trail fueled by the excitement and the sheer pleasure of being on a mountain trail. Around 11,000 feet, oftentimes in an area dominated by Ponderosa Pine trees, a sudden, pounding headache and tightness in my chest would repel me as if I had bounced into an invisible force field. If I continued to force it, the monster would unexpectedly join me on the journey. Slowly at first, then with increasing momentum, the monster would weave invisible vines around my legs, constraining me and shortening my stride until I could barely lift my feet from the ground. To suddenly feel the return of the body over which

I had little control, especially out in the wilderness where I was vulnerable, quickened my learning curve.

When Parkinson's entered my life, it was as if my body and mind split into two entities, operating independently of the other. For years, the separation of the two made life challenging in ways that are difficult to describe to someone still in control of the simplest of bodily movement. However, since my recovery began I have slowly gained a rebuilt body that succumbs, for the most part, to the control of my brain.

Over many miles traveled as a lowlander, I had learned how to keep the monster in its cage, but being at altitude made its escape easier. Ironically, the monster helped teach me the better way to scale a mountain. I needed to listen to my heart during ascents. The pounding in the chest and loud drum beat in the ears do not seem consistent with the slow steady pace of the hike. As I learned to focus on isolating my awareness of breathing and heart rate, I also learned how to keep the monster at bay, by just keeping my pace steady and focus on the beating of my heart. When my heart rate increased to a noticeable level, I would stop on the trail until it slowed enough to fall below the awareness point. I moved up a trail until I became aware of the increase in heart rate, stop briefly, usually a period of one to two minutes, and then proceed, repeating the process over and over until I reached a summit. It was a form of interval training, and the more I repeated it, the less I had to think about it.

Over time, I was able to go farther between the brief stops. Hiking in intervals became second nature for me on mountains. It also kept the monster in its cage for the most part. As we moved slowly across and gradually up Kilimanjaro, I followed my training and stopped briefly when needed.

For the remainder of the morning we trudged along behind Steven at a pace that seemed ho-hum for him and his assistant guides, but increasingly difficult for the group following. Although we moved over the boulder-strewn landscape only a few feet apart, it was a solitary march in between the frequent breaks. With each step it seemed like the temperature dropped and the wind beat down on us driving tiny bits of the volcanic earth into our faces, which made talking or hearing what was said difficult. I wore alpine sunglasses and a shemagh to protect my face. With the wind, the clouds seemed to move in all directions. Depending on the bends in the trail, the peak was either directly in front of us or to our left as we gradually moved eastward and uphill.

At the lunch stop, a short distance after the junction of the Machame Route with the Lemosho Route and before reaching Lava Tower, much of the food went uneaten. Everyone was experiencing some level of headache and mild nausea, which virtually eliminated hunger. Ibuprofen was the preferred main course.

The effects of high altitude on the body and brain in regard to nutrition and hydration are counterintuitive. When one needs to eat and drink to meet increased demands, the natural desire to do so is suppressed or delayed. Forced eating and drinking was necessary for the first, but not the last, time on our trek.

The climb was beginning to wear on each of us, but none more so than Bella. Even with more frequent stops to rest, her strength faded quickly and the nausea overwhelmed her. Unable to eat or hydrate adequately, the decision was made to get her to camp as soon as possible. An assistant guide led Bella down a separate, southern path used primarily by porters, which descends quickly to Barranco Camp, bypassing Lava Tower altogether. She was disheartened and by her need to cut the day short and move on to camp. Each of us hoped she would recover quickly and be able to continue the climb in the morning.

For much of the remaining distance between the lunch stop and Lava Tower, we saw the hulking chunk of rock in the distance. When we reached the base, we stopped for an extended break. At just more than 15,000 feet, there was higher ground looming above us and I wanted to go as high as possible. I asked Tyler if he was up for climbing to the top of Lava Tower, and he said yes with enthusiasm that matched my own.

When we approached Steven to get his input, he indicated that some climbers take the time to climb the tower, but it would add one to two hours to the day's hike. If we took the additional time at the tower, it could keep us from reaching Barranco Camp before dark. He wouldn't allow anyone to climb unless he led. A quick poll of other members of the group found that twelve of us wanted to make the climb. Kate, Ava, and Lizzie chose to remain at the base to rest. We left our packs behind, and Tyler, Noah and I broke out our GoPro cameras with head mounts, eager to capture the adventure.

The serious rock climbers who come to Kilimanjaro plan their route in order to camp at the lesser used Lava Tower campsite. From there, it was a short distance to climb the rock faces of the tower. For others, like those of us in our group, there is a simpler route to the top that doesn't require ropes, carabiners, draws, or harnesses. There are, however, several places where the use of both hands and feet are required to progress upward. At each of these locations, Steven went first instructing the group regarding hand and foot placement.

I asked the others if I could be the first to follow Steven. The old man of the group was also the most excited about the climb. As each of us reached the top of the mini-climbs, we joined to cheer on those coming behind us. Once the members of the group made it successfully, Dismass followed and we proceeded together to the next troublesome spot.

Forty-five minutes after we began, twelve members of the group and our guides, Steven and Dismass, reached the top of Lava Tower. At approximately 15,200 feet, we stood on higher ground than any peak in the contiguous United States (Stedman, 2010, p. 270). At first, the cloud cover enveloped us and the view was limited, but it quickly cleared to allow us views of the campsite below, the Arrow Glacier/Western Breach route leading to the summit to the north, the Shira Plateau to the west, and the Barranco Valley to the east.

After returning to the base of Lava Tower, Steven told us that only a small number of climbers attempt to reach the top, which wasn't exactly what he led us to believe before attempting the climb. In fact, although he had made more than a hundred trips up Kilimanjaro, he had climbed Lava Tower only a few times. He shrugged and said it was better to not let people know something is hard before actually doing it. Yes, I thought, I know a little something about doing things the hard way.

26

HOMECOMING

Some people spend an entire lifetime
wondering if they made a difference in the world.
Marines don't have that problem.

PRESIDENT RONALD REAGAN

I don't remember what I was doing when the call came and, for some inexplicable reason, I didn't check to see who was calling before answering. The weary voice on the other end of the line surprised me and spoke the words I had yearned to hear, instantly bringing me to my knees. "Dad, I'm done. I really didn't think I was going to make it, but I did. The last patrol is finished, and I'll be coming home soon."

The call was brief, but life-altering. The burden of seven months of uncertainty and the additional months of dread that came before were lifted in an instant. *I would see my son again!* Hope would soon become reality. I shared the news with Liv and Max and family and friends. We cried, we celebrated, and we rejoiced. It was one of the most jubilant days of our lives. I thought of all the other families who were experiencing the same emotions then I remembered those families who would never see their sons or brothers or husbands again. I prayed that God would heal their broken hearts. Not until much later did I come to know just how many times Eli had come close to joining the ranks of the fallen.

The last patrol wasn't special or much different from many others the Echo Marines had gone on, except for the fact that it was their last. That fact, however, made it more dangerous than many others. Just hours from completing the time in which they could come face to face with Taliban fighters, the Marines fought internal battles against being distracted or less focused while outside the wire. They set about their task, completed their mission, and eventually heard over their radios, for the final time, the order they had been waiting months to hear: Return to base. That's when things started to go sideways.

On three separate occasions during the return to their Forward Operating Base, Marines were wounded by IEDs, or Improvised Explosive Devices, one of them severely. Each time, the men tended to the wounded Marine until he could be medevac'd out for treatment then divided up his equipment to be carried back to base. Just as the remaining Echo Marines approached their base, the FOB came under attack by Taliban fighters, pinning them down in a no man's land of sorts.

After the firefight, my son saw his best friend standing on top of the high point of the base where the heavy weaponry was located, his arms raised in a "V" for victory. They had made it. They were done. Their mission had been completed.

Long after that day, when Eli finally felt compelled to share the story of the last patrol, he told me about something that had haunted him for some time. As a team leader, he walked point on patrol. He would not ask those for whom he was responsible to do something he wouldn't do himself. He told me that he had walked the same path as the three Marines who were wounded by IEDs. He had literally stepped over the IEDs before the men behind him were wounded by them. Why had he been spared? Why had he made it through combat physically unscathed?

Blissfully ignorant of the details of the last patrol and much of what Eli had endured during the deployment, our family set about making plans for his homecoming. It would still be a couple of weeks until the 2/9 returned to the States, but we made arrangements in a mad rush. Hundreds of other families similar to ours were making travel plans, and there always seemed to be a shortage of rooms in Jacksonville during homecomings. We decided to share a beach house with Sam and Nancy.

Located on Topsail Island about an hour south of Camp Lejeune, the beach house was what we hoped would be a perfect location for our sons to unwind during their first few days back home. We wouldn't know the exact day of their return until twenty-four to forty-eight hours before, so we booked the house for a week, hopefully giving us time before their arrival to be prepared and time afterward to spend with them.

We fretted about details like welcome home banners, buying fresh, new clothing for our son to wear while at the beach house and making lists of his favorite foods we needed to buy. In our own way, we were learning how to unwind and relieve the crushing pressure we had been under for months, days, and hours on end. It was finally time to allow ourselves a chance to sweat the small stuff and look to tomorrow without the tunnel vision that had crippled us for so long.

The road home from Sangin in the Helmand Province of Afghanistan is a long one. The Marines of Echo Company first traveled from their Forward Operating Bases to the Main Operating Base in the area then on to Camp Leatherneck, the largest Marine Corps base in Afghanistan and the temporary home for more than 7,000 troops. With each move, they carried more than a hundred pounds of gear and endured hours of waiting before continuing. Compared to what they had come through, it wasn't a big deal, but it gave them the opportunity to vent, gripe, cuss, and unwind.

Upon arrival at Camp Leatherneck, they were able to bathe thoroughly with hot water for the first time in more than six months and eat real, hot meals. It was during the few days spent at Camp Leatherneck that Eli was promoted to the rank of Corporal. From there, they began a series of flights, the first of which took them to Kyrgyzstan. Located in Central Asia on China's western border, the former Soviet Republic was home to Manas Air Base near the city of Bishkek.

Opened in late 2001 to support Operation Enduring Freedom, it was a main transit point for United States forces coming into and leaving from Afghanistan, and for those of other International Security Assistance Force (ISAF) members. Once out of the Afghanistan war zone, the Echo Company Marines had a few days to decompress before continuing their journey home.

From Kyrgyzstan, battalion companies flew in waves to somewhere in Europe where they would either refuel or change planes. The location didn't matter to them, since they couldn't leave the airport, but at least they'd be able to say they had been to whatever country they landed in. Upon leaving Europe, their next stop was Marine Air Station (MAS) Cherry Point in North Carolina. Finally, they boarded buses for the hour-long trip down the coast to Camp Lejeune, where their families awaited their arrival.

Sam and Nancy drove from their home near Dallas to our home near Birmingham. As our sons were slowly taking the legs of their trip home, we began our journey to where we would meet them. Together we left for Topsail Island the next day, arriving just minutes before the kickoff of Super Bowl XLV, Packers vs. Steelers. When we finally crashed into our beds for the night, we had no news regarding their anticipated arrival.

Sixty hours later we sat in a gym at Camp Lejeune with hundreds of other Echo Company families awaiting the arrival of our Marines. One of my two best friends since childhood, Rivers, drove down from the Washington, D.C., area the evening before to welcome Eli home. He and his wife had been with Liv and me at the hospital for Eli's birth more than two decades earlier. It seemed appropriate that he was with us to welcome Eli home.

The nervous energy inside the gym was as palpable as the biting cold outside. Children ran about and played while adults sought updates about the final miles of Echo Company's trip home, the anticipation building with each passing moment. Notices were given when their plane landed at MAS Cherry Point, when they began the bus ride to Camp Lejeune, upon their arrival on base, and when processing and turning in their weapons at the armory had begun, which was our signal to join those family members who had braved the elements all morning. The wind and the cold bit deeply, and it seemed fitting that the families should endure one last small hardship before embracing our loved ones.

The families filled a hundred yards of sidewalk across the street from the gym, looking away from the street at a courtyard lined on two sides and across by barracks. Family members held banners and homemade welcome home signs while we waited for the moment when we would first see our Marines. From a pathway between barracks, the dull browns and gray of winter first gave way to the bright red of a guidon, the company standard emblazoned in gold with the Eagle, Globe and Anchor in the center, "USMC" across the top, "2/9" in one bottom corner, and an "E" in the other. On the morning of February 9, 2011, Echo Company, 2d Battalion, 9th Marines, came marching into the courtyard in formation behind the guidon. As they marched into view, stopped, then stood in formation, I couldn't help but notice that some tattered, colorful blankets, rolled tightly and strapped to several of the men's packs, had made the return trip home with them.

When they were dismissed and broke formation, the cheers of the families filled the air and like runners at the start of a race, hundreds of people ran to find their Marine. Within seconds, Rivers, Liv and I were surrounded by the sights and sounds of reunions: joyful screams, tearful embraces, and smiles ... so many smiles. Max had set off on his own to find his brother, and after a few minutes of confusion and not seeing Eli or Max in the crowd, they found us. As Max approached us then stepped aside, Eli came walking through the crowd behind him. If only a photo could capture the magic and the love of a mother as she embraces her first born son when he returns home from war. The image of her holding him, her love almost visible as it surrounded him, is one forever etched on my memory, as is the smile on Max's face as he stood watching the same moment in time.

When it was my time to greet my son, he looked at me with bewilderment. The man who stood before him looked like the man he had known in his youth, much thinner, standing straight with no cane in his hand, the weariness of years of struggle replaced by vigor and joy. I grabbed the back of his neck and pulled him close. I barely noticed the smell of sweat and the soil of a foreign land still embedded in his uniform as my tears were added to the mix. All I knew was that I was finally holding my son. I could touch his face, look into his eyes, and hear his laughter. My son was finally home.

27

VOLUNTOLD

Iron sharpens iron,
and one man sharpens another.

PROVERBS 27:17, ESV

O nce the screams and tears of joy subside, once the hugs and kisses and smiles captured in photos or video become memories, and once the welcome home banners are discarded or tucked away as keepsakes, the war raged on in Afghanistan and at home. For the families of servicemembers, it's as if the war ends once our loved ones return home, and we can stop holding our breath and go forward with our lives. A combination of naiveté and wishful thinking, we want to believe that we can love them back into the world they knew before war and everything will be okay. However, the reality lies deep below the surface, invisible to the world, but completely real nonetheless.

Since the wars in Iraq and Afghanistan began, the number of suicides by active duty personnel and especially among young veterans has risen at an alarming rate. We didn't want our son to become a statistic. Liv and I were sensitive to the issue. We knew that one of Eli's friends, a newlywed Marine in his unit, had taken his own life after returning from a deployment to Iraq two years earlier. His brother Marines not only grieved, but were troubled that they had missed their brother's subterfuge as he hid the signs of desperation.

The signs of the invisible wounds were subtle at first, especially since our time spent with Eli after his homecoming was limited to a few days immediately following his return, a short family vacation, and a brief home leave. Liv and I thought it would help him to begin transitioning back into civilian life by being involved in honoring the fallen and helping his wounded brothers. During the last month of Eli's Afghanistan deployment, I began fundraising for a well-known veterans charity organization, involving friends, family, and local businesses and churches to support programs to help wounded veterans. A community event was planned for early spring, when Eli would be home on leave.

Many in our community gathered for a memorial walk. Thousands of dollars in donations were raised to help wounded veterans, but more importantly for Eli, he was able to see that his friends' sacrifices mattered to civilians. It was a solemn day for him, yet it seemed to help him take a small step forward.

He was often moody and tired with only brief flashes of happiness during our times together. Of course, we didn't expect him to be the serious yet fun-loving person he was before going to Afghanistan within just days of returning, but as the days stretched into weeks and months, Liv and I began to realize just how deeply wounded he was and the task before us.

He was physically home, but he had left parts of his heart and soul in Afghanistan, and survivor's guilt was eating him alive. Just as we had done when he was learning to walk as a toddler, we took him by the hands and walked beside him as he came to grips with his war experience and helped him in any way we could. *Your son needs you to meet him where he will be.*

Eli completed his active duty service and left the Marine Corps during the summer of 2011. In just four years, he had seen two wars in two countries and experienced extensive combat in Afghanistan. He had fulfilled the vow he made after 9/11, when as a twelve-year-old boy filled with love for his countrymen, he had sworn to fight the enemies of our country. He had seen many brother Marines die or be horribly wounded, and was facing the departure of his younger brother for the Marine Corps, where he could possibly one day meet the same fate.

Max graduated from high school just weeks before Eli left the Marine Corps, and had received word that he would be leaving for basic training onboard Parris Island in September. Our sons tried to spend as much time together as possible during the summer, essentially passing the baton of service from one to the other. As their parents, Liv and I struggled with the dual tasks of helping the son who had come home and letting go of the son who would take his place. We both needed strength, and found it primarily in the deepening of our faith and the freedom that came with the furlough from my physical prison.

Although we had survived dissimilar ordeals, Eli and I were both at similar places in our lives. We were looking at unexpected futures, wondering why we had survived, and for what purpose. For long periods of time, neither of us had expected to survive the battles we faced, yet here we were, still standing, with the smoke clearing and wondering, "What now?" I had focused all effort into being physically ready for my son's return home, but I wasn't prepared for the flood of questions that came with my unexpected physical renewal.

From an analytical perspective, I tried to convince myself that my brain had found new ways to work around the Parkinson's, although at the time I couldn't find other cases of people experiencing such a dramatic regression of symptoms. Could it be just the exercise, change in nutrition, or a change in attitude? I added up all the pieces, yet the equation never balanced. God had spared me for a purpose, and my healing had a Divine element. It was one I couldn't quantify or explain, but real and conditional.

I found that if I stopped moving for any period of time longer than was needed for essential rest, I became symptomatic. It helped me see that the same was true for Eli. He, too, had to move forward to heal. I could help him break free of the inertia and be caught up in the draft toward healing. In order to move forward, I needed a goal that would drive me and be of interest to Eli. I found it in an unlikely place and in a number: New Mexico and 26.2.

I bounced around some ideas and searched the Internet for an athletic event that would both interest Eli and give me a goal far beyond my immediate reach. I considered several of the obstacle course event series and locations. I made casual inquiries during conversations with him, thinking he might be motivated to do some event with Max before he would leave for basic training. Eli wasn't interested in mixing it up with a bunch of civilian weekend warriors. He had been through the real thing and was a real warrior. The taste, smell, and adrenaline of war can't be matched by an athletic event that's difficult for those who haven't risked their lives to achieve victory.

Pay dirt lay deep in one of my many searches. When I read about the event, it struck a chord deep within me. It was far beyond my current athletic ability and had two elements that I knew would be of interest to Eli: a military theme and World War II history. The Bataan Memorial Death March, a marathon-distance endurance hike held annually at White Sands Missile Range near Las Cruces, New Mexico, commemorates the courage and sacrifices of 75,000 American and Filipino soldiers. The Bataan Death March, which took place in the Philippines in April of 1942, was one of the worst atrocities in the history of war.

In 1989, members of the ROTC department at New Mexico State University began sponsoring an event to honor the memory of many New Mexico natives and their families who were deeply affected by the death march. A few years later, the Army and the New Mexico National Guard began sponsoring the event, and it was moved from the campus of NMSU in Las Cruces to White Sands Missile Range, and has grown from the initial 100 to more than 6,000 marchers annually. Although primarily a military event, many civilians choose to take part to honor a family member or friend who has served during a time of war (Bataan Memorial Death March, 2015).

The number 26.2 invaded and occupied my consciousness. Before Parkinson's, I had never considered going 26.2 miles, running or walking. The only time I had ever enjoyed running was a lifetime ago when I had a football in my hands trying to get one more yard. After the intense battle with Parkinson's and in the early phases of my unexpected recovery, I was drawn to endurance activities. Finding my limits and pushing through them became part of my new identity. My newest goal was set. I would march in the 23rd annual Bataan Memorial Death March in New Mexico in the spring of 2012, and I would bring Eli with me. He just didn't know it yet.

When I presented the idea of marching the Bataan event with him, he was reluctant. Throughout his growing up years, Liv and I tried many ways to motivate Eli to take what we considered to be the proper course of action. We praised him and we corrected him, we rewarded him and punished him, all to no avail. His fierce independent nature was extremely difficult to tame, and we were often exasperated by our inability to reach him once his mind was made up. He had a well-developed conscience. His sense of right and wrong drove him, and there was little anyone, including his parents, could do to persuade him to take a different course of action if he believed he was doing the right thing. His childhood to adult quest to become a Marine had been the paramount example. His Achilles' heel, however, was guilt. He simply could not live with it.

He seemed so lost trying to come to grips with his war experience in his post-war world, I had to do something to draw him out and give him a goal in the future to work toward. I don't believe any parent likes to use guilt as a means to motivate their child, but if it's for the child's benefit, a parent will resort to extreme measures in the heat of the moment. The conversation wasn't exactly enjoyable, but it accomplished the goal.

"I've decided to train for and participate in this event out in New Mexico," I began.

"Pops," he replied with the tone of denial, "I'm happy for you, that you're able to go do stuff now, but whatever it is,

I'm not going with you to New Mexico to jump over stuff and crawl through the mud with a bunch of people who don't understand what real hardship is."

I countered, "Son, it's a military-oriented, marathon-length hike through the New Mexico desert with thousands of civilians and active duty and veteran military, not a mud run or obstacle course."

"Oh, yeah, really?" he replied, dripping with sarcasm mixed with a fit of laughter, "Dad, I've humped it all over Iraq and Afghanistan in arid, desert environments because I was following orders. Do you really think I want to go do the same here in the States? You are nuts, old man."

Slightly wounded and angered by his dismissal, I stated my case. "Son, after all I've been through, this could be something really significant for me. We've supported you with all we have, and I'd like for you to be there with me to experience something I never expected to be able to do. I don't want to do this alone. I want to experience this victory with you. Do you think you can't make it 26.2 miles?"

He hung his head in mock defeat and replied, "So, you're pulling out the big guns, huh? You're guilting me into going with you? It must be really important to you to do that. OK, pops, I'll go. I've just been *voluntold*. You'll have to get ready for it alone, though, because I'm ready to hump through any desert anywhere in the world. Just name the time and place." End of discussion.

Although he wouldn't admit it, I had found his hot button and pushed it. He wasn't just guilted into doing something he didn't want to do. I had dug deep and found his competitive spirit. More directly, I had touched on that which exists in every man, the desire to compete against his father. Whether a match of wits or athletic prowess, it is something that we can't resist. Steel sharpens steel. Eli and Max had felt it necessary to hold that desire in check, at least the physical part, for most of their teen and young adult years because of my fight with Parkinson's.

Perhaps our conversation had ignited a long-dormant need in him, whether he realized it or not, and I was prepared to take full advantage of it. If I'm honest with myself, I found something unexpected in our conversation as well. It was the desire to compete or measure myself against the man Eli had become, someone whom I respect and admire greatly. He is the best parts of both his mother and me.

28

KILIMANJARO:
DAY 3 - A DIFFICULT DESCENT

26 AUG 2012

After reaching the top of Lava Tower, both the physical and emotional high point of our day, the Machame Route descended to an elevation just above 13,000 feet. Climb high, sleep low. It's supposed to be a relatively easy hike of less than three miles down through the Barranco Valley where giant groundsels, found only at high altitude on the mountains of equatorial East Africa, dot the landscape along the trail to Barranco Camp at the base of the Barranco Wall (Stedman, 2010, pp. 271-272). It was an easy hike for everyone but me.

While descending into the Barranco Valley, the monster attacked without warning, and in a matter of minutes I became fully symptomatic. The legs I had grown accustomed to working again faded and the nearly useless ones returned. Every step I took on the rough and rocky path during the descent was a struggle, so falling and sustaining an injury became the immediate concern. Even as I struggled, the analytical part of my brain kicked in. Cause and effect. What had triggered the monster's sudden return?

Will, Dan, Tyler, and Dismass held back from the rest of the group and walked beside me, wanting to help, but I initially resisted. My teammates formed a protective barrier around me to catch me should I fall. Dismass was especially alarmed, because he was unaware of my battle with Parkinson's and thought I was suffering from altitude sickness. As he was preparing to go on to camp and get help for a medical evacuation, my teammates explained my situation to him. Fortunately, he understood about Parkinson's and relented. For much of the remainder of the climb, he would be my shadow.

Frustrated and exhausted, the filter between my thoughts and my spoken words failed me at one point during the descent, and I shouted out, "I just want to be normal!" I didn't realize I had spoken the words aloud until Dan reassured me that I had never been normal. As an adult, I had never wanted to be normal or average until I thought I could no longer be at least normal or average. It wasn't until the difficult descent that day and hearing Dan's quip that I began to question what being normal really meant.

My earliest recollection of wanting normalcy stemmed from the stormy, sometimes violent, relationship with my father. Why couldn't I have a normal dad who wanted to play ball in the backyard instead of berating me at every opportunity, as if it were a sport? Years later when Parkinson's entered my life and literally destroyed most of what I had worked so hard to achieve, when my legs and left arm didn't work properly and my head bobbled uncontrollably from side to side and up and down drawing unwanted attention, I had desperately wanted to be normal.

When my recovery began, being obedient to God's direction to get up and walk, to meet my son where he needed me to be, drove my actions. As my physical health improved, I realized that I had a deep, personal yearning to at least appear normal, even if I wasn't. As I regained more and more control over my body, I came to grips with the fact that no matter how normal I seemed, to most who knew me or discovered that I had Parkinson's, there was always an asterisk. No matter what I achieved, there was always the "not bad, or that's great ... *for a guy who has Parkinson's." Why couldn't an achievement just be an achievement?

The five of us made it to Barranco Camp after darkness and the cold had enveloped it. The glow of the meal tent called to us. Even as I put on a happy face and declared victory over Parkinson's to my teammates during our evening meal in order to allay their concerns, doubt had taken up residence in my mind for the first time since the climb began.

As I lay in my tent that night at the base of the formidable Barranco Wall, the next obstacle to overcome in our quest to reach Uhuru Peak, I was exhausted and virtually immobile after the day's struggle. The words I had shouted in desperation bounced around in my mind. *I just want to be normal!* Earlier in the day, several of my teammates and I had overcome our fears to climb Lava Tower, but the day had ended once again trapped in the body that had been my prison for eight years. Although I had prepared and trained vigorously, I was left wondering if my body would cooperate and allow me to continue the climb in the morning. The connection between brain and body felt tenuous at best.

The contrast between the day's events was a microcosm of my life to this point: A consistent stream of highs and lows, great blessings I had never deserved and struggles that had taught me how to fight against and overcome obstacles. Humbled by the epiphany, I finally understood that normal doesn't exist. We are who we are, a compilation of extremes.

My personal quest for normalcy was laid to rest during the night. There is no "normal" for me. I am both the prisoner and the free man, the man who lies weak in the valley and the man who stands on summits few have reached. The experiences of the day solidified the realization that all of us are both wounded and exceptional in some way. We are all owners of an asterisk.

29

JUMP

Your soul may belong to Jesus,
but your ass belongs to the Marines.

EUGENE B. SLEDGE

No youngest child likes to be called, or even thought of as, the baby of the family, especially the youngest male who is within days of leaving home for Marine Corps basic training. I couldn't help it, though, and neither could his mother. To us, Max had always been a miracle child.

Eli had come to us so early in our marriage, we had assumed that having our second child would be just as easy. It wasn't. There was much heartache to be endured before Max entered this world. Two pregnancies ended in miscarriages between the births of our oldest and youngest children. It wasn't until Liv reached the seventh month of her pregnancy with Max that we began letting our guard down and believed that we would soon be able to hold our second son.

When he came to us, he was perfect and so strikingly different from his older brother. Fair-skinned with blond hair and blue eyes, the physical differences weren't the only thing that set him apart from Eli. Even when small, Max wasn't the typical youngest child. His calm demeanor and quiet self-confidence was ever accompanied by his toothy smile. He always came across like a tiny adult. Although it seemed at times that both of our sons had the typical personality of an oldest child, one trait common among youngest children was evident. Max had always looked up to Eli and wanted to follow the path his older brother had blazed, and to prove that he could do anything his brother could do.

Deep down, Liv and I had known for most of the previous decade that Max would one day follow Eli into the Marine Corps. Whenever older brother said he was going to grow up to be a Marine, little brother chimed in with, "Me, too!" There was a time during his teen years, after Eli had left home, that he purposefully tried to be different from his older brother, but the phase soon passed. As he approached adulthood, he couldn't be who he wasn't. Competing against his older brother was part of his nature. He, too, would serve our country. He, too, was determined to earn the Eagle, Globe, and Anchor. Our sons would not only be blood brothers, but also brother Marines.

When the calendar page turned from August to September, Liv and I knew we had only days left with our youngest child before we would be left alone as a couple, back where we had started more than two decades before. Our time with our children at home seemed to have gone by so quickly, now that we had time to reflect on our lives together. It was a somewhat melancholy time for Liv and me, but Max was about to explode at the seams with excitement to be beginning his adult life on his terms. Good, bad, or ugly, he was eager to find out what he was made of. In a twist of irony, he would get on the bus that would take him to Parris Island on the tenth anniversary of the event that had led his brother to make a decision that altered the course of our family's history.

I wanted to do something special with Max before he departed, and told him to just name it and we would do it together. I wasn't prepared for his reply, but I had no choice but to comply. Not only was I about to see my youngest child leave home, apparently, I also had to jump out of a perfectly good airplane with him before telling him goodbye. I knew it was something he had wanted to do for quite some time, and when presented with a "just name it" opportunity, he was going to use it to get some long-planned, good-natured revenge on his old man before leaving home. He knew I had always been scared of heights, and could barely contain his pleasure as he watched the blood drain from my face. I reluctantly agreed.

We made a long weekend of the adventure. We would jump at a drop zone on the outskirts of Atlanta, then travel to Tennessee to see extended family and a football game at Neyland Stadium before leaving home for basic training the next day. He didn't believe I would actually follow through with it, right up until the moment he watched me exit the plane strapped to a tandem skydiving instructor. My son gave me one of the best gifts I've ever received: an opportunity to face one of my greatest fears and overcome it. Few experiences in my life have changed my perspective so drastically or so quickly. I've rarely felt so free.

On the morning of September 11, 2011, we woke early and watched the solemn tenth anniversary ceremonial reading of the names of those who perished in the attacks. Afterward, we left our home and went for an early Sunday lunch before the post-church crowds descended upon the local restaurants. When finished, we left the restaurant but didn't return to our vehicle. Instead, we entered the Marine Corps Recruiting Station a few doors down where we said our goodbyes, hugged him tightly, and watched as he and several other recruits boarded a van that would take them to Montgomery. Once there, he would then board a government bus to South Carolina where he, like his older brother before him, would become a man.

30

MARATHON DISTANCE

Cades Cove, Tennessee
Great Smoky Mountains National Park

October in the Great Smoky Mountains National Park is a beautiful yet busy time. People from all over the country flock to the park that straddles parts of Tennessee and North Carolina, to enjoy the colorful array of leaves while also hoping to catch a glimpse of the wildlife. More than nine million visitors a year pass through the park in autos, on bikes, and on foot, which is double the number of visitors of any other national park (National Park Service, 2015, "Statistics"). As a native Tennessean, it has been part of my consciousness for as long as I can remember.

Deep within the park is Cades Cove, a remote valley in the Tennessee portion of the national park steeped in both Native American and pioneer history. It is the most visited destination in the park (National Park Service, 2015, "History of Cades Cove"). Millions of visitors a year follow the eleven-mile, one-way, paved touring loop through the valley. Several

structures built in the 1800s, including churches and homesteads, remain along the loop offering tourists a glimpse of
settlers' lives.

During peak season it can take up to four hours to drive
the loop in clusters of bumper to bumper traffic as people
stop to take photos of the old churches and homesteads or
stare in awe at the sighting of wild turkeys, deer, or even a
black bear. Sitting in a car is not the best way to experience
the beauty that exists in this special place. Only a few choose
to walk the loop through the valley, and on this day I would
be one of them.

Since the day I set my sights on the goal of hiking 26.2
miles at the Bataan Memorial Death March, I had been in
training. I began carrying a backpack stocked with essential supplies and some additional weight to make the training more difficult. It was one used by Eli in Afghanistan. I
branched out from the lake trail to walk every hill and street
in our large subdivision.

As spring turned to summer then summer to fall, I reached
new milestone after milestone. Twelve miles became fifteen,
seventeen miles then twenty. In the months since I had taken
my first steps into an unexpected recovery, I was becoming
more accustomed to my renewed abilities. After years of being
less than able, it was a joy to be able to go farther and do more
than I had ever attempted before Parkinson's entered my life.

Cades Cove was a little more than an hour's drive from
my hotel room in Knoxville, and I planned to begin the hike
just before daybreak. Per the training schedule I had created and had been following religiously, the goal for the day
was to hike twenty-two miles, or two laps around the eleven-
mile-long loop. The plan was to train up to hiking twenty-five

miles before the Bataan march and save the accomplishment of reaching the 26.2-mile goal for the actual event. As the first few miles passed and the darkness began to give way to the early glow of day, I began thinking about going the entire distance.

My legs had been my physical strength my entire life before Parkinson's made itself known, but over the years since, I had forgotten what it had felt like to walk normally without struggle. One doesn't truly appreciate the simplest things in life until they're gone, and the hope of regaining that which was lost doesn't exist. I felt the power in my legs surging downward into the pavement, propelling me forward with each step. *I'm not supposed to be able to do this*, I thought over and over again.

Although I wouldn't understand it until much later, I spent a lot of time wondering, as did my family and friends, how it was possible that I could have relearned to walk after so long. My recovery seemed so sudden to them, but they weren't the ones living in my body experiencing the daily, incremental changes. I was the one who had documented and charted each step and every mile, and was able to see not only the gradual increase in distance but also the steady increase in walking pace.

My newfound ability to walk appeared normal to others, but I knew it was different from before. The brain is complex and fascinating, and its ability to find ways of compensating for damage or loss of ability, in my case the loss of dopamine producing cells, is remarkable. It wasn't until a few years later that I gained some insight regarding the physical mechanism that had allowed me to relearn to walk. I saw a video report about a movement disorders specialist at the Mayo Clinic in

Jacksonville, Florida, who had taken wheelchair-bound patients with Parkinson's and taught them to walk again with the aid of a walker equipped with a visible laser beam (Reuters, 2014).

Although I don't fully understand the processes in the brain that are triggered by the visual cue to step over the light of the laser, I believe that a similar process allowed me to relearn how to walk. I realized that what I had assumed was a lingering symptom of Parkinson's, a slightly stooped posture, was actually something else. Although I look ahead when walking, I don't look farther than will allow me to see my feet. As long as I can see them moving in the bottom field of my peripheral vision, I can walk with ease. I was doing just that as the mist that had settled over the valley during the night began to rise and dissipate with the warmth of the rising sun.

Much of what I had set out to do and had accomplished had been for the benefit of my sons, helping Eli move forward after his war experience and inspiring Max to be his best. Today was different. For the first time in a long time, I claimed this day and what I would accomplish for myself. The distance I would go would be done without Parkinson's medication. While on the drive from Alabama to Tennessee, I had peeled off the small patch that delivered the lone remaining medication, held my arm out of the open window, and let the wind take it from my hand.

The medications had enabled me to combat Parkinson's, yet had done so at great cost. As I slowly weaned myself off the Parkinson's meds over the past year, I realized how much better I felt and began to understand that much of the endless grogginess, fatigue, headaches, and compulsive behavior had been byproducts of the medications. To go meds-free had been more of a process than a discernible decision. I needed to know what living with Parkinson's in its raw form would feel like. I didn't know what to expect out here on this historic path, but I was excited to find out.

At the halfway point of the loop is a rest area with restroom facilities and a small store that sells a few snacks and all sorts of souvenirs and park-related memorabilia. I had hiked 5.5 miles before I sat on the porch of the old store and ate a carb bar.

The day was shaping up to be a glorious, beautiful day in the Smoky Mountains. The fall colors, warm sun, and moderate temperature made for one of those rare experiences when all the variables line up perfectly. I felt great, so my stop was brief. I was eager to move forward and see what the day would bring. Somewhere between the rest area and the completion of the first loop, I decided that this would be the day I would reach the ultimate goal of 26.2 miles. Although six months ahead of schedule, I realized I shouldn't waste the perfect setting and location for the sake of keeping to a training plan. The time was now.

After a lunch/rest break at my truck parked by the entrance to the loop, I began the second lap. It seemed odd to walk the same path during a different part of the same day. Memories of the familiar landscape seen just hours before had a distant and timeless quality. The silence and stillness of the early morning had departed, along with the dampness. The winds of fall now moved through the colored leaves of the trees and moved white, puffy clouds swiftly through the perfect blue sky above the valley.

I walked against the slow-moving traffic as cars and trucks from Alabama, Kentucky, and Virginia, among others, stopped and started again and again in a miles-long train around the loop. Kids waved, while a few adults just stared in disbelief that a man would bother walking the road instead of sitting in the comfort of an automobile. Others didn't notice me until their cars were within feet of me, making me hastily consider whether or not to jump from the pavement into the tall grass or ditch beside the road. Still others looked at me with longing as I walked, perhaps thinking about a time when their bodies could carry them with ease through a wilderness or along a country road. My stride was still strong, and there was little doubt that I was moving at a higher rate of speed than the traffic moving in the opposite direction.

I was mildly surprised when I glanced at my watch and realized it had been twenty-four hours since the last dose of medication, yet I still felt good. I wondered if it was the sheer beauty of the day that was carrying me along, seemingly unaffected by my constant companion. "Constant companion," I said out loud, as if it was the beginning of a new way of thinking about Parkinson's, a transition of sorts. It had been the monster, the tormenter, and the prison guard.

There were moments during the long, lonely days of suffering after my career was lost when I asked God why he had set me apart, like a book, placed high on a shelf after a reader has lost interest. I had spent so much time in the figurative wilderness of the unknown, both my own struggle and the months spent not knowing if my son was alive or dead most of the time. In the months since my recovery began, I had spent hours alone by choice, training my brain and body to work together as one again.

There are people who believe being alone in the wilderness reveals character, while others believe it builds character, and will argue their stance based solely on opinion rather than experience. Over the years, I had become an expert at being alone for hours on end, and my experience had taught me that it does both. Spending time alone in suffering reveals our weaknesses, while spending time alone working toward goals that are far beyond our grasp builds character. We try, and we fail. We learn, and we try again. When we succeed, we are able to measure the growth, and move forward with the awareness that we can succeed, that we can stretch our limits and have victory built upon defeat.

I felt the toll of the day's effort as I neared the end of the loop for the second time adjacent to the stables and the meadows where horses grazed and ran free. Unmedicated, my legs had carried me twenty-two miles, which had been the original training goal for the day. I was tired, but it was more a natural state earned by taking nearly fifty-thousand steps rather than the lack of dopamine in my brain.

As I sat on the tailgate of my truck while stretching my back, now free of the pack that had seemed to grow heavier throughout the day, I took in the beauty surrounding me. The late afternoon sun shone through the fall colors, and the breeze seemed to pass through me. The aroma of a cookout coming from the picnic area nearby awakened my raging hunger. I felt so good, and wanted to lay down in the grass and sleep the sleep of one who's earned it. But I couldn't. Instead, I strapped on the pack, stuffed some fruit in my mouth, and began walking toward the entrance to the loop.

Two point one miles back the way I had come twice before, turn around, and hike back to the truck for the third time in one day. It was all I had left to do to reach the goal I had sought for months, though it seemed like ages. Every step of the distance between twenty-two and twenty-four point one miles was a struggle. I counted off every tenth of a mile on my GPS watch, and each felt like a mile instead. When I finally reached the turnaround point, I knew I had made it. Even though a little more than two miles remained, I knew I would make it to the finish. My body was on autopilot as I celebrated every step toward accomplishing my goal.

Ten hours and a few minutes after I had begun, the digital readout on my GPS watch showed 26.2 miles, and I stopped within feet of the picnic area where a large group of people were finishing their cookout. I asked the person closest to me to take a photo with my phone, and he kindly obliged. As the sun was setting, I raised my arms in victory and the moment was captured.

Fifty-four weeks after I had taken the first steps from my prison of eight years, I hiked 26.2 miles in one day. My recovery was tangible and it was real. God had enabled a man who had fought for years just to take the next step to go the marathon distance. As I drove home that evening, basking in the warm glow of satisfaction, the reward for having accomplished a long sought after goal, I had the sense that it was just the beginning of something more.

The future that had seemed so dark and treacherous for so many years was gone, replaced by the promise of the great unknown. Later, after a hot shower and meal, I lay in bed physically exhausted yet not quite ready for the day of victory to end. I realized that I was fascinated with life and with living again. A childlike enthusiasm enveloped me, and my last thought before succumbing to sleep was, *What comes next?* I didn't have to wait long for the answer.

31

KILIMANJARO: DAY 4 - BARRANCO CAMP

27 AUG 2012

When I awoke, I could feel the echoes of doubt from the day before when my brain and body had failed me. I was still lying in the same position as when I had fallen asleep while unable to move. The question of whether I would be able to function was partially answered when my arms and legs obeyed the commands my brain was sending.

Just because I could once again move, it didn't keep me from having a surly attitude. I was angry that my constant companion had once again asserted itself as my foe. It felt like I couldn't escape the monster and hated being in my own skin at times. I had fought for so long and so hard to push it below the surface, to be able to do whatever those with me on this climb could do, and yet the monster had exposed me to everyone.

Even though I had made peace during the night that my long-held idea of what is normal doesn't exist, I didn't want to see the doubt on the faces of my teammates when I emerged from the tent. I had been so confident that I had Parkinson's under control and that it wasn't a problem in regard to the climb, yet alone in the cramped confines of the tent, I was consumed by my own doubt. Would my brain and body commit the ultimate betrayal and keep me from reaching my goal? Why was climbing this mountain so important anyway?

Jolted from the self-imposed torture going on in my mind by the sounds of the camp coming to life, I grudgingly began the routine of preparing to leave the man made cocoon and join the others outside. As I partially stripped and bathed with baby wipes, I was once again reminded that had I not taken the road that had led me to this place, I would most likely be dead by now.

The tattoo of a phoenix on my upper arm reminded me that I was indeed alive. My son had taught me that every tattoo has a story behind it. Having multiple tattoos is common for most war fighters of his generation. They get them for several reasons. They served as a roadmap of their battles, to memorialize the fallen, or to remind them of why they do what they do. The thought of getting one had never crossed my mind until Eli asked if I would get one if he made it home from Afghanistan. I couldn't say no.

Just a few days after Echo Company returned from Afghanistan, I sat in a bustling tattoo shop full of young Marines in Jacksonville, North Carolina, not far from Camp Lejeune, and got my first ink. The artist was meticulous and professional as he pushed the image into the skin of my left upper arm. It was a skull, its face partially covered by an

American flag bandana, with two USMC KA-BAR knives crossed behind it. Eli's name was written on the blade of one, the other reserved for the day when Max had earned his Eagle, Globe, and Anchor. To my son, there was no greater way I could have honored him.

I got the phoenix tattoo on the first anniversary of my alive day for dual purposes: As a symbolic representation of my recovery from the ravages of Parkinson's, and as a daily reminder to rise above the ashes of doubt and the disappointment of inevitable setbacks. On this morning, it reminded me of just how far I had come. I had been losing the battle for years, but the tide had turned and I had climbed both symbolic and real mountains to make it to this point.

I cursed the part of my mind that had allowed doubt to gain a foothold and resolved to put the previous day behind me and do what I had been doing since my recovery began. Move forward. Rather than moving downward into a darkness over which I had no control, I would continue to move forward into the light.

The next twenty-four hours would have a tremendous impact on my future, one way or another. If I didn't make it to the summit, it wouldn't be because I gave up. Properly recalibrated, I quickly completed preparations for the day's climb and exited the tent. What I saw took me back nearly three decades.

32

AMERICA'S MOUNTAIN

Chasing angels or fleeing demons,
go to the mountains.

JEFFREY RASLEY

I was barely seventeen years old the first time I fell in love. It was definitely a case of love at first sight, and my heart and soul have been entranced since the day I first saw her. After teasing me from afar, the full measure of her beauty was finally revealed when the distance between us was eliminated.

I'll never forget the first time I saw Pikes Peak. She towered nearly eight thousand feet above me and dominated the city below and the plains that extend eastward for miles. As the chartered bus that had brought our church youth group from Tennessee to Colorado moved north on I-25 from Pueblo toward Colorado Springs, I caught glimpses of her summit trying to hide behind the smaller mountains that rise below her to the south. As the interstate entered the city near Fort Carson, her profile became more prominent. When we reached the heart of the Springs, her majesty was fully revealed.

When the bus stopped, a throng of hungry teenagers rushed the fast food joint. Our chaperones, church leaders and a few parents, must have worn the same exhausted and desperate look they'd had dozens of times over the course of the trip as they ushered the group into the restaurant: Like someone trying to herd cats. I stood alone in the parking lot looking up, my hunger momentarily forgotten, completely mesmerized by the mountain. I felt as though I was looking at the throne of God, and all those who moved about the city below were His children playing at His feet. Never before had I felt such a calling to climb a mountain. I vowed that one day I would reach its summit, and I would do it on my own legs.

Our meal break apart from the bus was far too short, and once again the bus moved north for Denver where we would turn to the east on I-70 toward Kansas and eventually home to Tennessee. I sat at the rear of the bus so I could see the mountain, finally losing sight of it near Castle Rock, where the view of the Front Range and the mountains beyond become more prominent in the distance to the west.

Growing up in eastern Tennessee, I had always had a connection with mountains, but had not laid eyes upon one as large and majestic as Pikes Peak. I knew I would return one day. Eventually, I would fulfill the vow I made that day as a hopeful, naive teenager. The storm I would pass through in the years before finally standing on its summit would only make the experience much richer.

More than a decade later I returned to the mountain, this time with my family. Less than a month after Max was born, we escaped to Colorado from our home in Texas during a holiday weekend. Many things in my life had changed since the first time I stood at the base of the mountain, yet the mountain remained the same. If we did nothing else during the short trip, I had to go to the top of the mountain.

Long before the upper half of the Pikes Peak Highway was paved, we zig-zagged up the mountain on the loose gravel road with no guardrails. I was scared out of my mind. One wrong move would send me, along with my beautiful little family, plunging thousands of feet to our deaths below. My heart raced as I white-knuckled the steering wheel. The warmth of late spring in the city below turned to the cold of winter with each passing mile up the mountain.

Two feet of snow awaited us at the peak, and the clouds that surrounded it robbed me of the view from the summit I had eagerly anticipated. It was also the first time I experienced the odd sense of claustrophobia in the outdoors, brought about by the thin air at 14,110 feet above sea level and made worse by the fast ascent via an automobile. Nevertheless, I stood still in the snow for several minutes, somehow believing I was physically closer to God at this elevation than I had ever been before.

After a quick snowball fight with Eli, Liv demanded that we leave the mountain. Her motherly instincts were sounding the alarm. She realized that it was crazy for our small children, especially a newborn, to be at high altitude. We made a hasty descent down the mountain, slowed only by the mandatory checks for overheated brakes. I knew I would return one day, but I didn't know nearly two decades would pass before I would set foot on the mountain again.

Years later, after returning home from Cades Cove where I had gone farther on my own legs than ever before, I began thinking about going *up* in addition to going *far* (Mt. Everest and Mt. Kilimanjaro are prime examples of *up*, but I had to be realistic at this point). The Bataan march was six months in the future, and I knew I was ready for the event well ahead of schedule. The financial commitment required to climb any of the Seven Summits was well beyond my reach. Realistically, no place better defined *up* than Pikes. It was within the realm of possibilities, but still distant. I could dream, though, and I did.

One evening in late October Eli came to visit while I was sitting at the dining table studying the history of Pikes Peak and the primary route to the summit, the Barr Trail. Between his move to an apartment in Birmingham and his new job, Liv and I had seen little of him for a few weeks. He seemed to be doing better adjusting to his post-Marine Corps life, and trying to figure things out. He wanted to go to college, but wasn't sure what he wanted to study. We ate dinner and Liv and I enjoyed a nice evening together with our son. It was surreal to have this normal family time together with him after all that each of us had been through not so long ago. After Liv turned in for the night, I wanted to show Eli what I was working on before he left, but he had other plans.

As we sat at the dining table with paper and maps of Pikes Peak scattered about, he took off his happy face and spilled what was troubling him. He spoke quickly, like a dam had broken, and asked that I not interrupt before he could let go of the tangled web of thoughts that filled his mind. I listened, and my heart broke all over again with the knowledge that his seemingly normal life was just a facade. I didn't know how to help him until he finished with the statement, "Dad, I can't seem to find the line that separates war and my future."

I understood why dreams of Pikes Peak had invaded my mind in recent weeks. God had been leading me to this moment, to the place I would once again meet my son where he needed me to be. Just as Pikes had changed something in me decades before, it could do the same for my son. I told him I had a plan, and that he needed to trust me. We were going on a road trip, and we were going to climb the mountain together. I hoped the beauty he would find in Colorado would displace some of the horrible memories he carried with him daily in his post-war life. He didn't know where else to turn or who he trusted more than his old man, so he agreed to go. The road trip and the mountain would soon change both of our lives.

33

ONE LAST MISSION

It is hard to fail,
but it is worse never to have tried to succeed.
In this life we get nothing save by effort.

THEODORE ROOSEVELT

Officially, we were in the middle of nowhere when I pulled off the pavement and onto the barren shoulder. Eli got out of the truck first and I joined him, both of us leaning against the front bumper. Neither of us spoke and the silence was uninterrupted for quite some time along the lonely, desolate highway somewhere in the northeastern corner of New Mexico. There was nothing special about this particular spot in the middle of nowhere, except the view.

As a small child, Eli had been to the mountains we were looking at, but had no recollection of it other than a few family photos taken during our brief excursions to Colorado long ago. Like countless people before him, he wouldn't forget the first time he saw the Rocky Mountains.

Most likely, it was the bitter cold November air cutting through us and across our faces that caused our eyes to water to the point of tears, but it could have been something deep in both of us rising to the surface. For me, it could have been seeing a lost love again after sixteen years apart. For him, it could have been feeling so alive in the presence of such beauty after all he had witnessed in a war-torn country halfway around the globe. Eventually, we blamed our wet eyes on the bitter cold and sought refuge inside the warmth of the truck.

Our road trip had begun two days earlier, and we had already seen and experienced much. We had left Birmingham on Sunday night and stopped in the capital of Oklahoma just before sunrise. We walked beside the Reflecting Pool at the Oklahoma City National Memorial as the sun rose, the eastern Gate of Time casting shadows across it, and the Field of Empty Chairs representing the lives lost in the attack.

Just a child when the attack occurred, Eli was deeply moved by the memorial. He had served his country in response to the terrorist attacks that had followed six years later, and had sworn an oath to defend the Constitution of the United States against all enemies, both foreign and domestic. It was only natural that his patriotism would swell in the location where the worst act of domestic terrorism had taken place.

After a stopover in Amarillo for the night, we made our way into northeastern New Mexico, where the open spaces helped him to begin to unwind. Long stretches of road with only brief reminders of humanity passed beneath us without a spoken word. For him, that we were together exploring new places was enough. Eli would soon see the mountain we had come to climb from the same vantage point as I had almost three decades earlier. He would see the same mountains of the Front Range come to him as they and I-25 grew closer together with each mile we traveled north.

The late autumn sun was setting as we reached the southern edge of Colorado Springs, and Pikes seemed to reach into the heavens as clouds consumed the peak, hiding it from view, teasing us. That evening we ate bison for the first time, bought the last few items of cold gear we would need for the climb, and readied our backpacks, gear, and clothing before hitting the rack early.

I was already awake when the 4:30 a.m. wake up call broke the silence in our room. Other than a few caveman grunts and hand gestures, conversation was virtually non-existent as we dressed, cleared the room, then pointed the truck west where the lower trailhead for the Barr Trail sat awaiting our arrival just above the Cog Railway Depot.

Completed in the 1920s, the Barr Trail is one of the most popular and most challenging trails in the Pikes Peak region. Surveyed and built over a period of several years by Fred Barr, an avid outdoorsman and entrepreneur who led burro trips up the mountain for tourists in the summer months, the trail covers thirteen miles and gains approximately 7,500 feet in elevation between the lower trailhead in Manitou Springs and the summit.

It's amazing how little we knew regarding what we were about to attempt. We had some basic knowledge about the history of the trail, had studied both trail and topo maps, had checked weather reports, and knew we had appropriate clothing and gear for the climb, but neither of us had hiked or climbed at high elevation before. Our bodies were just beginning to acclimatize to the elevation of Colorado Springs, and we were about to double that plus a couple thousand more feet. We had some basic knowledge, but we had no experience hiking in the Rockies. That is what made it an adventure: facing the unknown, pushing our bodies, and discovering our capabilities.

Ours was one of only a few vehicles in the parking lot at this early hour. Apparently, a few others had gotten an earlier start using headlamps to light their way. While waiting on Eli to let me know he was ready to begin, I sat on the tailgate of the truck, looking up at the steep switchbacks that marked the beginning of the trail.

Just fourteen months earlier, I had been a crippled man in the most dreadful time of my life, physically and emotionally. I could not have imagined climbing one of the tallest mountains in the United States, or more specifically, the same mountain that had captivated my imagination so long ago. How could thoughts of something so incredible have existed in the midst of the battles we were fighting? Yet here we were, alive and together, preparing to climb to heights greater than either of us had ever attempted on foot. We weren't just a couple of lowlander tourists out for a tough hike, we were two men searching for the ends to our wars. After coming through the darkest times in our lives, we were father and son, walking side by side into unexpected futures, both of us hoping to find our purpose.

Deep thoughts came to a screeching halt when Eli stepped in front of me. We were both dressed in black base layers, black and gray lightweight pants, jackets, and beanies, and black cold weather hiking boots. It was our uniform of choice.

The whites of Eli's eyes and his broad, toothy smile were the only recognizable features behind the mask he now wore.

While I had been reminiscing, he had carefully applied camouflage face paint using waterproof paint sticks and the application techniques he had learned in the Marine Corps. The base layer of light green lay beneath the slightly zigzagging brown and shades of deep green. The darker colors were applied to the naturally oily parts of his face, and the light colors on the shadow areas, working the light in such a way to help hide his facial features.

The only sound in the stillness of the early hour was my laughter. Even as I asked, "What in the world, son?" I knew it was perfectly Eli to the core—the boy he had been and the man he had become combined in one action. I saw both the mischievous grin of the boy and the serious eyes of a warfighter before me.

"One last mission, dad," he said, suddenly serious. "It's a rescue mission. This time, it's to find myself on this mountain."

"What about the looks you're going to get from the people on the trail?" I asked, fairly certain of his forthcoming reply.

"I don't care if someone think I'm nuts," he said, a half-truth at best. He *wanted* them to think he was crazy, to be repelled by the mask he wore, and so that he could find the humor in their shocked double takes when the recognition of something so out of place registered in their brains.

"Today is about us, just you and me," he said. "That's all that matters." That was the whole truth. We donned our packs and started up the trail. We hoped it would take us to the place where we would mark both an end and a beginning.

34

KILIMANJARO: DAY 4 - BARRANCO WALL

27 AUG 2012

While the majority of our group made it to Barranco Camp just before dark the previous day, the last remnant of light succumbed to darkness just as our small contingent entered camp at the base of the wall I couldn't see. As my legs began to fail me, my sole focus had been placing each foot on the next rock and the trekking poles in a position to help prevent a fall. Neither I nor those teammates with me had our headlamps in our packs, and the sense of urgency to reach camp before dark overwhelmed me. During the descent down into the Barranco Valley to camp, those ahead of us had seen what I now saw.

Everything about the climb had been difficult—the fundraising, the training, the preparation—so it wasn't a surprise that the next challenge was a literal wall. Rising nearly 800 feet above camp was the Barranco Wall, which stood between our current location and Kilimanjaro's summit (Stedman,

2010, p. 273). There wasn't a choice. We had to climb it. In climbing terms, it's a scramble, meaning no ropes or other climbing gear are required to scale the wall, but we would be using our hands in addition to our feet to reach the top.

As I looked around the camp, I realized how large and crowded it was. The Machame, Lemosho, and Umbwe routes converge here. Porters and trekkers from other groups were trying to move quickly to get in line for the single file climb up the wall, although not an easy task at approximately 13,000 feet. Our group would not be near the front of the line.

Several of my teammates had been wondering if I would be able to continue the climb, and were pleasantly surprised when they saw me moving about camp with a normal gait. They were kind by not voicing their concerns, and gracious with their smiles, handshakes, and hugs.

After three full days and nights on Kilimanjaro, none of us felt our best. Each of us had been worn down in some way by the mountain. The lack of quality sleep and the altitude made us feel like we'd been on the mountain for weeks instead of days. Bella was still battling persistent nausea. Will hadn't felt well since the afternoon before, but complained to no one. At the breakfast gathering, he said he may have gotten an intestinal bug during his week in Tanzania prior to our arrival. Dan had a mild but persistent cough. For others, old sports injuries were acting up. No one was talking about giving up, but I wasn't the only one carrying the additional weight of doubt.

After wrapping up breakfast, we gathered our packs with trekking poles stowed for the scramble ahead of us, and headed to the base of the wall. Up until this point in the climb, we had had only brief encounters with other groups as they passed by us or us by them, mostly during rest breaks. This morning was altogether different. Climbers and support crews from three routes converged at this point, and the wall is a natural bottleneck. The climbing route was easy to discern as a colorful, zigzagging line of climbers moved slowly up the wall ahead of us.

As the wait to begin climbing the wall stretched on, I thought about where I expected to be by this time tomorrow. The wall was just the first of many obstacles we would face in the next twenty-four hours. To reach the launch point for the final ascent, Barafu Camp, we would have to scale the wall and then cross several valleys while slowly climbing more than 2,000 feet in a counter-clockwise direction around the south side of the mountain. The weather would make it more difficult as periods of rain, sleet, and snow were expected at higher elevations later in the day.

Our time at Barafu Camp would be short before beginning the final ascent around midnight. I wouldn't allow myself to think about the following long day of descent while running on nothing more than the excitement of having reached the goal. I didn't dare think about the safari after the climb was completed, or going home next week. Reaching the summit was the terminus of my thoughts, and had been so for the past seven months.

Although I hadn't given voice to my thoughts to anyone, especially Liv, I had long ago realized that I was willing to die during the summit attempt if that's what it took to finally defeat Parkinson's stronghold on my life and declare victory over it. I had never felt more compelled to do something in my life. It was that important to me, yet I still didn't fully understand why. Maybe it was sheer spite. I would rather forfeit my life in the attempt for something great than succumb to the disease that was killing part of my brain every second of every day. As the line of climbers began moving, calling me back into the here and now from faraway places in my mind, I rebuked the thoughts of dying on the mountain. Doubt was feeding the forbidding thoughts, but I was still very much alive, and I had a mission to fulfill.

Of approximately 35,000 people who attempt climbing Mt. Kilimanjaro annually, the number who die on the mountain is extremely small. The estimated number of people who die while climbing Kilimanjaro each year ranges from 3-7 (exact numbers from the Tanzanian government are difficult to obtain), in most cases from acute mountain sickness (AMS) and falls, and, in some cases, from hypothermia (Climb Kilimanjaro Guide, 2015, "Facts"). According to the Climb Kilimanjaro Guide website (2015, "Altitude Sickness," para. 44-45), "There are two conditions associated with serious AMS, each of which occurs when fluid leaks through the capillary walls either into the lungs (this is called High Altitude Pulmonary Edema – HAPE) or into the brain (this is called High Altitude Cerebral Edema – HACE). Both conditions are rare but almost always occur because of ascending too high, too fast, or because one has stayed too long at very high altitude."

Kilimanjaro is considered by many expert climbers to be the easiest of the Seven Summits. However, the success rate hovers around only fifty percent. Hundreds of climbers are medically evacuated down or off the mountain each year. The large number of casual, unprepared climbers, who think it's easy and do not train specifically for the climb, bring the success rate down. In addition, the relatively fast ascent times,

5-7 days, leave less time for acclimatization. For comparison, climbers on Mt. Everest take approximately twenty days to trek to Everest Base Camp, which is at a lower elevation than Uhuru Peak (AlanArnette.com, 2015).

The morning was crisp and clear. As we moved slowly up the wall on the narrow trail that disappeared at times while climbing short, vertical sections of lava rock, we had ample time to look back down the valley at Barranco Camp and some of the wall we had traversed. The line of trekkers and porters extended as far as I could see below us. It was cramped quarters on the wall, and the starts and stops seemed to go on forever. Climbers stopped and squeezed up against the rock face to allow porters to pass by. Many times, I heard various forms of "excuse me" or "sorry about that," as movement came to an abrupt halt resulting in a teammate's face bumping into the rump or legs of the teammate in front of them.

After a few hours of up and down and sideways movement, our group reached the top of the wall. The weather changed quickly as we approached the end of the scramble. We stopped for a rest break before moving on to the next way point at Karanga Camp, hoping to look out from the top of the wall and be rewarded with a stunning view. Rather, clouds had engulfed the area where we now stood. It was as if we could step off the rock into oblivion.

We celebrated at the top of the wall. There were plentiful congratulations, high-fives, hugs, and pats on the back. We had tackled and overcome the last big physical and mental obstacle in our path before making the final ascent. It would be the last time all sixteen members of our group celebrated together.

35

DEMARCATION LINE

Everybody needs beauty as well as bread,
places to play in and pray in,
where nature may heal
and give strength to body and soul alike.

JOHN MUIR

The wiry, extremely fit octogenarian was moving swiftly down the Barr Trail when we met at a turn in a switchback. With a lifetime of experiences in her rearview mirror, apparently little could shock her. She didn't even do a double take when she saw Eli's painted face. She just smiled like she was welcoming us into her home, which is precisely where she was.

Rather than moving quickly past us with a bewildered look, as a small group of cadets from the Air Force Academy had done earlier, she stopped to talk. She asked where we were from and how far up the trail we planned to go. When we told her that our plan was to reach the summit, she smiled as she shook her head with the familiar gesture meaning, "No."

She told us that a snowstorm was brewing at the summit of Pikes, and it would most likely make its way down into Colorado Springs by sunset. With an air of quiet authority, she asked that we trust her. She explained that for more than four decades she had made a monthly journey up and down the Barr Trail, reaching the summit more often than not. Today was one of the few times she wouldn't. She knew the mountain and she knew the weather, and she advised us to go no farther up the trail than would allow a safe descent back down to the trailhead before dark.

Before moving on in opposite directions, we thanked her for the information and assured her that we would heed her warning and follow her advice. As she turned her back to us, she said, "I hope you find what you're looking for." Whether it was her standard farewell when encountering others on the trail, or if she had some keen insight, I'll never know. Although disappointed that we wouldn't reach the top of Pikes on this climb, Eli and I understood that it wasn't really important. We would find our own summit.

The clearing was less than a mile from Barr Camp, the unofficial halfway point of the Barr Trail. We had gained nearly 3,000 feet in elevation over six miles of trail to reach this point. Eli needed a break, and the clearing was the perfect place to stop for rest. We had caught glimpses of the mountain's peak as we hiked the trail, but from this spot we had a clear view of it.

Eli was disgusted with himself as he sat down in the snow and leaned against a tree, facing the peak. He had taken up smoking as a young Marine, and although he wanted to break the habit, he had yet to find success in doing so. Combined with his lack of physical training since he left active duty months before, he just couldn't get enough air to keep pace with me the higher we climbed. I was twice his age, and had spent years of my life barely able to walk, yet he was the one sitting, trying to get enough oxygen into his lungs while I was still standing, ready to go onward. In addition to feeling mentally and emotionally broken, he realized that his body was fading away as well. Sometimes, we need to feel completely broken before we are able to heal.

We spoke little at first, then not at all. As the minutes passed, we watched the mountain as the snow clouds hovered slightly above then consumed the peak just as the near absolute stillness and silence consumed us. Wilderness surrounded us. We could see the clouds moving, and hear the wind as it swept through the trees. But in this place, there was not a sound from nor any visible sign of humanity apart from us.

My son and I had had totally different traumatic experiences, yet we shared some of the common aftereffects. He had lived through tours at war in foreign lands, set apart from everything else going on in the world. I had lived through years of solitude, at war with my own body. It was difficult for us to believe that others could truly understand the battles we fought, with the similarity uniting us and serving as the basis of understanding.

He had been trained to be hypervigilant in all situations, resulting in a keenly developed situational awareness built upon extremely sensitive hearing and sight. The slightest sound or movement triggered a learned action or a reaction that he depended upon for his and his brother Marines' survival in the crucible of war. But there had been no way to turn it off since returning home. The hypervigilance that helped keep him alive in Afghanistan had become an affliction in the civilized world that the majority of humanity calls home.

Rather than my senses being sharpened, Parkinson's had taken some of my cognitive ability over the years, stripping me of much of my multitasking capability and forcing me to focus intently on specific tasks. Noise and visual distractions could break my train of thought, which was often followed by brief moments of confusion then agitation.

I understood the battle he was fighting, perhaps far better than he could comprehend. It was the after-the-battle fight that was tormenting him. Without his weapon, his uniform, and the closeness of those who shared his experience, he felt alone and ill-equipped in a world where his training worked against him. The noise of mass humanity and the speed at which civilization moves in a million different directions at any given moment had caused overstimulation of his senses to the point of burnout. Everything was a threat that had to be assessed, yet no action could be taken.

When I set out on the road to meet my son where he needed me to be, I had no idea of the destination or how long it would take to get there. I prepared and trained as if his life depended upon my ability to walk again and my efforts to be unbroken, to be remade into something new and something more. We had been destined to walk beside each other to a place where only one's legs could take him, which happened to be right to this clearing six miles up the Barr Trail. This place, where the beauty, the silence, the stillness, and the lack of any threat or judgment from humanity, was where he finally found the demarcation line between war and his future. He was completely broken, yet renewed at the same time. He was finally able to exhale and breathe in the possibilities of a life yet lived. It would not be easy, but the time had come for post-traumatic growth.

After our day on Pikes, we moved just a hundred miles up the Front Range to another world altogether. From the solitude of the wilderness the day before, we found ourselves in one of the most diverse pockets of civilization in the country: Boulder, Colorado. Undoubtedly, it is an exotic people zoo. As we walked the stone paver walkways amid the shops lining each side of Pearl Street, I could see the fundamental change in Eli's outlook. He was rejoining humanity.

Instead of being agitated or feeling threatened by the sheer number of people, sights, and sounds, there was a sense of *C'est la vie* as he observed college kids with pink hair walking the same street as old couples, families, businesspeople in suits, and many others of his generation. Here, he didn't feel different because everyone was different, and no one seemed to care. I doubt he would have felt totally comfortable having an in-depth conversation with a pink-haired college kid, but it was the concept that intrigued him. Even though he was changed by his war experience, there was a place for him in the civilian world, a place where he could thrive. He just needed to find it.

Our road trip took us west over the Rockies into Utah the following day. We spent a few days exploring the parks in the Moab area and Monument Valley and a day in New Mexico before making the final non-stop sprint back home. We spent nine days on the road and covered nearly four-thousand miles traveling through ten states. Together, we experienced much of what my son had fought for and what our flag represents: vastly different landscapes and the different, yet similar, free people who inhabit them. But it was in a small, still, quiet clearing on a mountain trail where we both found the unexpected and the hoped for.

For more than a year, my mission had been meeting him where he needed me to be. On the mountain that had held a special place in my heart since long before Eli came into the world, a goal had been met and a mission partially fulfilled. It was so similar to letting go of a child's bike and watching him ride alone for the first time. There are few gifts a parent can give a child as precious as freedom.

Just as he had found an end and a beginning, so did I. There is a clarity of purpose found in the peace between the two that can alter one's trajectory. Eli discovered that a purpose for his life existed beyond war, even though he was yet to understand what it may be. I realized that God had rebuilt my body and my mind for more than just the purpose of helping my son.

It was on Pikes where I found something else, something that would become an essential part of me. I saw that there are others who were struggling, others who needed someone who had pushed the rock and climbed the mountain to show them it was possible for them. I didn't know their names nor could I see their faces, but I knew they were out there. Because of the road I had traveled, I was uniquely prepared to meet them wherever they were on their journey, and I would help them find ways to overcome, ways to climb their mountains.

36

COMMITTED

The mountains are calling and I must go.

JOHN MUIR

Colorado wouldn't leave me alone. Throughout the holiday season, the festivities surrounding Max's graduation from MCRD Parris Island in January 2012, and the continuing training for the upcoming Bataan march, thoughts of Colorado were never far from the surface of my consciousness.

Could we leave the place where we had built our lives during the past twelve years? Since returning from the road trip with Eli, Liv and I talked about it often. We had been tumbleweeds in our twenties and early thirties, willing to go just about anywhere for opportunity. Although it had taken some time at first, we had formed lifelong friendships and work relationships with people in Alabama. In addition, after several years of not wanting anything to do with organized religion, we had found a church home where we were forging new relationships that enabled us to grow in our faith.

For so many years we had tried not to think much about the future, instead learning to value our days together one at a time. My battle with Parkinson's and Eli's war deployments had taught us that the future was never certain, regardless of our plans or good intentions. Could we just leave all that was familiar to us behind to start over in a new place where we knew no one? We knew we were at a crossroads. We had to decide to stay the course with the familiar and comfortable, or shake things up and take what could be our last opportunity for new adventure.

Both alone with our own thoughts and together during many discussions, we always arrived at the same destination. Why would we do this? For what purpose would we walk away from all that we knew for the unknown? The answer came not in the form of a voice from Heaven, or some unmistakable sign showing us the way. It came from a most unlikely source, social media.

February began just as January had ended. I trained every morning, logging miles with a loaded backpack in preparation for the Bataan march. I arrived home, grabbed something to eat, and opened my laptop to read some online articles before hitting the shower. A blog post by The Michael J. Fox Foundation captured my attention. Team Fox, the Foundation's community fundraising program, announced that they were assembling a team to climb Mt. Kilimanjaro in late August (The Michael J. Fox, 2015, "Foxfeed Blog: Kilimanjaro").

A few months earlier, I had read about a group of men who had inspired me to continue my newfound passion for mountain climbing. The three men, amputees from three separate wars and two different generations, summited Mt.

Kilimanjaro in 2010. I came across their story while researching the Bataan Memorial Death March. They had participat-
ed in the march earlier in 2010 as part of their preparation
for Kilimanjaro.

Sitting there in the kitchen, I felt a strange sense of *déjà
vu*. I had experienced what I was feeling before, and it took
a few moments of thought to understand. Just as I had intui-
tively known on the morning almost a decade earlier when
my legs failed me for the first time, I knew that I was living in
a new reality. I had a deeper understanding of why my body
had been restored and for what purpose I had been training,
specifically for endurance activities. Although I did not yet
understand why it was so important, I knew I was meant to
climb Mt. Kilimanjaro.

My head was swimming as I first sent an e-mail, then called
the Team Fox contact person to get more details. I discovered
that a rather substantial minimum fundraising goal was required to be part of the team. If I didn't meet the goal in the
allotted time, I would be required to meet the goal myself.
It was money that we didn't have, and I had no idea how we
would pay for travel or any of the other expenses. The fundraising projects, first raising money to buy and send blankets
to Marines in Afghanistan, then raising money for Wounded
Warrior Project, had prepared me for what was to come next.
It was time to enter the arena and join the fight to find the
cure and defeat my adversary once and for all.

Even as I discussed the crazy idea of climbing Kilimanjaro
with two of my closest friends, Jake, my former boss, and
Puller, the man who brought me to Alabama, I already knew
the path I would take. When Liv arrived home from work,
I pounced as soon as she walked through the door. I made

my case, presenting all of the info I had gathered throughout the day, unsure of her response. Her cross-examination went straight to the core of the matter.

"Do you believe that this is what God is leading you to do, that it is what you're meant to do?" she asked. She did not ask "Do you think you can make the climb?" or "Do you think you can raise the money?" She had asked the most important question first.

Without hesitation, I answered, "Yes."

"Then it appears you are going to Africa," she said, as she was finally able to set her purse and coat down and fall into the comfort of her favorite chair that had eluded her while I had stated my case. We talked late into the evening about what would come next. The decision to climb Kilimanjaro triggered the decision to leave behind everything we knew and move to Colorado. If I was going to have a chance at making it to the highest point in Africa, I would need to train on the mountains, to train at altitude.

More than twenty years after she first fell in love with the young man with dreams and the confidence to pursue them, once again she said yes when I asked if she believed and was willing to come with me into the unknown. This time, though, we had more than two decades of history together. She had witnessed and been part of living out the dreams, and understood the sacrifice and commitment it takes to chase them. Perhaps her greatest comfort and my reborn confidence came from knowing that this time I was following God's direction instead of striking out on my own. This time, there was no doubt that God's fingerprints were all over what we were about to do.

37

A WALK IN THE DESERT

Bataan Memorial Death March
White Sands Missile Range, New Mexico

After a year and a thousand solitary miles of training, I was finally among my herd. The bright lights shone down on the soccer fields where nearly seven thousand marchers gathered in the hours before daybreak. The largest American flag I had ever seen hung from the long arm of a crane and snapped and popped with the gusting desert wind. The sight of it penetrated my soul as we found our designated pre-march staging area on one of the country's largest military installations, White Sands Missile Range.

Eighteen months after my Alive Day and a little more than a year after Eli returned from Afghanistan, we stood together as we watched the young and old, the fit and not-so-fit, the able bodied and those with missing limbs gather at the eastern base of the Organ Mountains in southern New Mexico, ready for the start of the march. We were joined by my lifelong friend, Rivers, and a new friend, Davis, a Marine Corps veteran and longtime school teacher from Tennessee.

Although I had already proven to myself that I could hike the distance, the next fifty-two thousand steps would move me much farther away from the gates of my former prison than I could imagine. The desert would be a new and totally different challenge. Finally, I was just a few yards from the starting line of the endurance event for which I had spent hundreds of hours in training. More than that, I would once again walk beside my son and together we would mark a new milestone in each of our journeys of healing.

The day prior we had come to White Sands to complete the registration process and pick up our event packets. While in line, we discovered that several Bataan survivors, men in their late eighties and nineties, were on site giving brief lectures or question and answer sessions. From them we heard true stories of the savagery that occurred on the march up the Bataan peninsula and in the prison camps. Their stories of survival humbled me and made my battle with Parkinson's seem small, yet what I took away from their stories was what they did after their horrific war experiences.

In spite of their physical, mental, and emotional wounds, the survivors came home and built families and careers. Many led perfectly ordinary lives after returning home, and others became professors or legislators or successful businessmen who built organizations from the ground up. They had not only survived but had thrived after their traumatic wartime experiences. That point was not lost on either Eli or me as the sessions ended and we stepped out into the arid, desert environment.

We finished the day in Las Cruces before turning in early, rising much earlier than usual, and making the drive to where we now stood. The opening ceremonies began at the same moment the first burst of orange rose above the horizon and the jagged tops of the Organ Mountains emerged from the shadows behind the stage we couldn't see. Our view was blocked by the crowd that now filled almost every square foot of the soccer fields. We couldn't hear much either, but knew when to remove our hats for the invocation and to cover our hearts or salute for the playing of the national anthem.

The moment finally arrived to begin the march. First, dozens of wounded veterans moved out to the starting line. Men and women wore heavy packs and others had prosthetics, heavy packs, and even gas masks covering their faces. It was a hardcore bunch, and I was honored to share the same piece of real estate for the day.

Eli had been mostly silent since we woke. He's not a morning person, but as we moved to the start line I sensed that it was more than early morning malaise. I'd seen the look in his eyes before. He was thinking about his fallen brothers. He was shaken loose from his reverie with the loud boom of the howitzer that marked the beginning of the march. Davis, Rivers, and I witnessed his immediate transformation as he came to life, as if suddenly aware that he was among thousands of others and adventure was afoot.

Just past the starting line, Bataan survivors were seated, waving to the marchers. As we passed by them, we returned their waves and thanked them as we continued onward. As we snaked our way through the compound and out into the desert, we walked due east directly into the rising sun. The brightness and warmth seemed to foretell of a day with endless possibilities. With each step, I was not only moving farther away from the prison that had held me for so long but also closer to the highest point in Africa.

By mile five of the march, our foursome had split into two pairs. Davis and I were lagging roughly fifty yards behind Eli and Rivers. Although I couldn't hear their conversation, I could see that Eli had come to life and enjoyed catching up with Rivers, one of my closest friends, the man he'd known his entire life, the man who'd been there for his birth and his homecoming and many other occasions in between. Suddenly, they stopped and Eli reversed directions, coming back to me at a jog.

"Hey, old man, you need some help?" He yelled, as if he was talking to one of his boots, or new Marines.

"Don't worry about me, son, I've gone this distance before and I know how to set the pace," I yelled back, feigning aggravation.

"Yeah, well, I don't want to have to carry you later, *old man*," he said, oozing mock disdain rather than endearment.

I shooed him away as I kept walking at the pace I had set for the first five miles. I watched as he relayed our exchange to Rivers, then as Rivers turned to look back at me and laughed. In another five miles, Eli would learn why I was moderating my pace. At mile eight, we would stop at an aid station and hydrate, then leave the dusty desert path and join a short section of the paved road we had driven much earlier that morning. By mile ten, we would be on the miles-long ascent up into the Organ Mountains.

I thought I could crush him on the hill. I had been training on hills in Alabama and Tennessee for the past year. Eli relied on his youth and Marine Corps experience. It felt good and right to be out here competing with my son. It was good to feel confident and strong and focused out here in the desert, far removed from my prison and his battlefield where every step could have been his last.

Eli responded to the challenge as he matched my stride and we pulled ahead of Rivers and Davis. Rivers could have beaten each of us up the hill. His job with a federal agency requires that he stay in excellent physical condition, which wasn't an issue as he'd been a workout junkie his entire life. He chose to match Davis's pace, which was slower because of foot problems.

We stopped at the mile ten aid station halfway up the incline to hydrate and set down our packs for a few minutes. We noticed a young veteran who was Eli's age sitting in a chair near the aid station. A double amputee, he was doctoring the remaining stumps while his prosthetic legs sat to his side. His pain was evident, but the grit, focus, and determination on his face inspired us to move forward once again. I had no doubt that medics would have to drag him from the course while bleeding out before he would quit.

As we moved up the remaining two miles to the point where the course would leave the paved road to encircle a mountain known as Mineral Hill, once again Eli and I moved ahead of Rivers and Davis. Both of them said to go on. They knew how long and hard I had trained for this event and didn't want to hold me back.

Eli was wearing most of the gear he had used in Afghanistan, including his desert frog combat shirt, boonie hat, and desert tan CamelBak backpack. Added to his Marine Corps gear were tan hiking pants and boots, and a full beard.

With pieces of his combat gear on and his sleeves rolled part way up revealing his tattoos, he was unmistakably a Marine Corps combat veteran.

Several times we passed by young soldiers, sitting on the shoulder of the road rubbing their feet and complaining about blisters or their heavy packs or both. According to Eli, they were obviously boots who had yet to deploy anywhere in the world. Each time he would slow down, and with subtle authority would ask the young soldiers if they needed food or water or assistance … and, with a mischievous grin, he would then ask if they needed a Marine to carry them up the hill. Each time he would receive the one-finger salute or a fit of cursing in response from the young soldiers. Not to be outdone, they would grudgingly leap to their feet and rejoin the march. Interbranch rivalry was alive and well out on the course.

At the halfway point, near a training site consisting of a group of makeshift buildings that resembled a small village in Iraq or Afghanistan, we stopped again to rest and allow Davis to doctor his feet, which looked more and more like they'd been run through a meat grinder. He was in pain, but determined to go on. Trained as a field medic, Rivers was concerned about Davis's wellbeing and wanted to hike with him in case he needed help between aid stations. Eli and I grudgingly ceded their request to go on ahead of them.

My son and I covered the miles of the dusty desert path encircling Mineral Hill, talking freely about our futures, enjoying the views from the mountain looking out across miles and miles of desert, the bursts of yellow desert wildflowers close by the trail the only color we saw other than muted shades of tan. We matched each other's cadence stride for stride.

Since his return from Afghanistan, we had climbed mountains together in the cold and snow in Colorado, stood under natural arches and on canyon rims in Utah, and now hiked side by side in the New Mexico desert. I enjoyed each step, and my gratitude for God's healing me so that I could do these things with my son filled me.

After completing the loop around the mountain, we stopped at mile eighteen to rest and hydrate where the dirt trail rejoined the pavement on the descent down the mountain. We decided to take a longer than usual rest break to see if Davis and Rivers would catch up to us. As Eli plopped down in the dry grass on the side of the road, he grunted loudly in pain. An unseen rock in the grass had gouged his hip.

When he tried to stand, he couldn't bear any weight on his left leg for several minutes. He resisted my help, and trudged slowly down the hill, every other step resulting in a burst of pain and a muffled grunt. He continued this way for the next three miles, until exhausted from the effort and the pain, he finally spoke the words that were so hard for him to say. "Dad, I need your help to finish."

This man I respected so much, but always the little boy that lived in my memories and my heart, needed me and was counting on me to rise to the occasion. He wrapped his arm around my shoulder and I reached around his back and gripped his good hip. Together we moved and rested, moved and rested, over and over again in true Bataan fashion. During my research of the Bataan Death March, I had seen many photos of emaciated men carrying their fellow soldiers this way. For the next five miles, it was if Parkinson's left me completely, as if my strength formed in my heart and restored dead brain cells to life, pushing massive amounts of dopamine throughout my body.

Finally, we reached the mile marker with the number 26 inscribed on it. We stopped briefly and asked a fellow marcher to take our photo. We were exhausted, but our smiles weren't fake. We had done it, together. Only 385 yards remained between us and the finish line. Walking side by side, we finished together as the sun fell behind the mountains to our west. He held back a step just before crossing the finish line, ensuring that I would finish before him.

Rivers and Davis crossed the finish line several minutes later, as did the young amputee veteran we had seen much earlier. After Davis received medical attention and we ate our post-march meal, we piled into the car for the trip back to Las Cruces. As we left the missile range, Eli proclaimed that it was one of the greatest things he'd ever done and couldn't wait to return to do it again. Although we were exhausted to the core from 26.2 miles hiked, a lot of healing had taken place during our walk in the desert.

The day in the desert was yet another turning point for me. I realized that I was no longer a crippled man who had escaped his prison only to be inevitably caught and returned. God had rebuilt me, using my love for my son to begin the change in my life. I was willing to do whatever He asked of me, to go wherever He wanted me to go. I knew beyond a shadow of doubt where I was meant to go next.

38

KILIMANJARO:
DAY 4 - TO BARAFU CAMP

27 AUG 2012

After three days spent trudging across barren, inhospitable earth above 10,000 feet, everyone in the group was worn down. Fatigued by the miles, the lack of quality sleep, and the ever-present nausea and headache, a dark mood seemed to settle over the group. The addition of the wet coldness, the pounding wind, the need for food combined with lack of hunger, and mind-numbing boredom didn't help matters much.

I was tired of being tired, and tired of being cold and wet. I wanted to bathe and to feel the warmth of the sun. I wanted to sit in a comfortable chair for a few minutes, and I really wanted a steak, or at the very least, a bacon cheeseburger. To escape, I tried drifting into that getaway spot in my mind where good food, the warmth of the sun, the gentle breeze, and the soothing sounds of the ocean exist. It worked for a little while, but the mental escape from my current circumstances was ever so brief.

There was no conversation as we moved eastward and subtly down the mountain to Karanga Camp, where we would stop for a brief meal before taking a hard left and then climb more than 2,000 feet to Barafu Camp, the launching point for the final ascent up the mountain. Heads down to avoid the pounding of the sleet and snow in our faces, we marched along in a single-file line, separated from one another by several yards.

Throughout the seven months leading up to the climb, I had never been more certain of my destination. I must reach the top of this mountain, no matter the cost, even if I don't fully understand why. Now, in this moment, as the cold fog that had enveloped the ups and downs of the small valleys, and alpine desert we were crossing turned first to ice cold rain, then to sleet, then to snow, questions persisted, demanding answers. *Why are you here? What are you doing? What is your purpose?*

The day after I learned of the Team Fox Kilimanjaro Expedition, I signed the fundraising commitment and became the third member of the team after my two teammates who are employees of the Foundation. Later that same day a for sale sign was planted in our front yard, and a sales contract soon followed. Any questions we had regarding the path we should take evaporated when we received an offer on the house after just three weeks on the market. When we put it up for sale, Liv and I knew that if we were truly following the path God wanted us to be on, things would happen to move us in the direction we should go. But neither of us had expected things to move so quickly. Upon return from the memorial march in New Mexico, we started packing and would move from Alabama to Colorado Springs by the end of April.

It wasn't until we were somewhere in Arkansas on I-40 West that the questions hit me with such force that I thought I would need to pull over to throw up. While driving the lead truck of a two truck and personal vehicle convoy, I could have sworn that one of the flashing road signs read, *"What have you done?"*

While driving the big, cumbersome moving truck across the country, I found myself suddenly scared out of my mind, questioning everything I was doing. I wanted to turn around, to go back to our home and reside in my comfort zone. But there was no going back. There was no turning around. The wheels were in motion, both literally and figuratively. All of our worldly possessions were in the trucks and Liv was already transitioning from working at the hospital to working from home.

What in the world am I doing here? Sometimes, I've known the question was coming, the inner voice asking if I am heading in the wrong direction, like a warning beacon in the fog. At other times the question comes as a surprise, like a spiritual earthquake threatening to crumble my convictions into a pile of rubble that must be rebuilt before I can move forward.

Our house was gone, and we were on our way to a place we had only seen on the Internet in a city and state where we knew not a single soul. We had done it just so I could train on the mountains of Colorado to prepare for climbing Kilimanjaro. It was no wonder that several friends and family members thought I was crazy when informed of our impending relocation. Liv and Eli were counting on me to lead our family in a new direction, and I had been so certain ... only to suddenly be having a meltdown in the middle of nowhere. Fortunately, I was somehow able to quell the panic, mash the gas pedal to the floor, and after a few days and a thousand more miles, we eventually arrived in Colorado.

The questions lingered in my mind as the group sought refuge inside the meal tent at Karanga Camp. Weather conditions kept the camp hidden until it suddenly appeared out of the wintry mixture. The tents and climbers from other teams were barely visible in the sullied light outside the tent, and there was little difference inside except for the lack of the rain/sleet/snow mixture hitting our faces. From their zombie-like appearance, I could tell that I wasn't the only one who had been wondering what in the world we were doing here.

We had been separated by several feet and the elements for the last few hours, each of us alone with our thoughts. Only inches apart now, crammed into the meal tent and huddling together for warmth, I looked into their cold, pale faces and tired eyes and was reminded of the answers. Drew and Annie were doing this to make a difference for their fathers, as were Grace and Noah for their father. Dan was climbing this mountain to honor his late father and to help find the cure so others wouldn't suffer as his father had. As I looked at each of my teammates, it was clear that something had driven and was continuing to drive them to be here in this moment. Doing something for others is a stronger driving force than doing something for one's self.

At first, climbing Kilimanjaro represented a rare opportunity to prove to myself and my family what could be done. It hadn't taken long to realize how the climb could impact others. As the team began to take shape, the Fox Foundation asked me to write a few guest posts about the climb for its blog. It is a common practice for them to feature people living with Parkinson's who are doing extraordinary things like running the New York City marathon, or in my case, climbing one of the Seven Summits, to raise awareness and funds for Parkinson's research.

Not long after the first blog post appeared online, I began receiving comments and notes of encouragement via e-mail and social media from others with Parkinson's. Their messages to me had a common thread running through them. They didn't know it was possible for someone like them to do something as daunting as climbing Kilimanjaro. They wanted, they *needed*, to believe it could be done. It mattered to them. In addition, as I approached individuals and organizations to tell my story and solicit donations for the Foundation, I found that others with no connection to Parkinson's were inspired by what we were doing.

My mind may ask why I am here on this mountain, but it's my heart that provides the answer. My life does have purpose beyond just existing. I began to see that opportunity had been brought about by my having walked the hard road. I had been in the storm and had come through it to the other side. Over time, I realized that what I was doing had a purpose beyond myself.

During those solitary years when I thought I had no purpose other than to merely exist while waiting to die, my world had been so small. It had been so difficult to think about the hardships that others faced. What would I have given for someone like the person I was becoming, someone battling the same enemy, to walk into my life and show me what was possible? Had that person been there for me, how much suffering could have been avoided, and how much hope for a new life could I have had? Yet, other than Michael J. Fox's example, there had been no one like that to show me the possibilities.

Parkinson's wasn't some cosmic accident that had randomly chosen me to torment. By design, it had entered my life to be my teacher and my mentor. I had to learn things the hard way to understand suffering and to develop a newfound, deep desire to help others. Climbing Kilimanjaro wasn't about showing others what I could do, it was an opportunity to show others what *they* could do. That by reaching the top of this mountain, I would have opportunities to connect with those in the midst of their struggles, to take them by the hand and say, "I am like you. Let me show you what you can do."

The fabric of the tent couldn't effectively keep the cold, wet mixture and the gusting wind at bay for long. We grew stiff and even colder while sitting, barely picked at our food, and said next to nothing during our short break at Karanga Camp. We were just a few hours from beginning the final ascent. None of us knew if we had it in us to make it to the summit, but no one wanted to quit. The world outside looked just as bleak when we exited the tent as it had when we entered. Grudgingly, we strapped on our packs and began climbing again. None of us really had a choice. We would continue to push against this rock. For whatever reasons drove each of us, once again we began moving in the only direction we could go: Up.

39

SUMMER OF SUMMITS

I lift up my eyes to the mountains—
where does my help come from?
My help comes from the Lord,
the Maker of heaven and earth.

PSALM 121:1-2, NEW INTERNATIONAL VERSION

I t had been an absolutely ideal day on the mountain, right up until the moment I had come upon the unexpected roadblock I was now facing. Without speaking, I cursed my luck with almost every unsavory word I could conjure.

Neither of us could look away for more than a second, and then only to quickly assess threats outside the small, intense universe we had unintentionally created. We were locked on, and neither of us was willing to give an inch of ground. Betting on the side of caution, I dared not instigate any quick movement, believing my adversary would move to fight rather than flee. For every small, cautious step I had taken forward, the beautiful beast had responded in kind until we now stood mere feet apart. We wanted to occupy the same piece of earth, if only for a second or two, but had been at an impasse for a brief eternity since our worlds had collided.

Both of us were defender and aggressor, although it was clearly understood that I was the invader. Our goals were simple: She wanted to defend that which was most valuable to her, and I wanted that which lay another thousand vertical feet beyond the kid she was protecting. The black, sharp-tipped horns protruding from her skull and the trekking poles I held in my hands were the tools of warfare should it come to that, but there was little doubt in my mind who would be the victor. I really didn't want my obit to read, *Idiot gored to death by a mountain goat.*

At first I had seen only the baby goat coming up the rocky cliff to one side of the trail, but I knew the nanny wouldn't be far behind. When two adult goats appeared with the kid, it seemed a perfect photogenic moment with majestic wildlife against the backdrop of the barren terrain and a perfect blue sky. The two adults were both female. Their short beards and the patchy remnants of their external coats this late in the year made their gender easier to determine.

I saw beauty, but the mother goat saw me as a threat and moved aggressively down the trail toward me, stopping thirty feet away. Over the course of several minutes, we took part in an especially slow dance. One step up on my part resulted in one step down the trail by the goat, the gap slowly closing until we could hear the other breathe. With the sharp drop-off to my left and a field of ankle-breaking rocks to my right, my only viable options were to retreat down the trail or to keep moving forward.

I hadn't packed my gear the night before, then risen at two a.m., then driven for three-plus hours, and then climbed more than two-thousand vertical feet up this mountain to be turned back by anything short of the heavens opening up and raining bolts of lightning down upon me, yet, here I was, unable to proceed for some time because a mountain goat stood in my way. Part of me wanted to laugh at the ridiculousness of the situation, while another part wanted to kick rocks and curse the sky. A solid case was being made for the belief that God does indeed have a sense of humor. But the longer I stared into her eyes, the more I understood just how beautifully symbolic the situation was. She was a living, breathing example of the challenges I had faced blocking my path forward, the shedding of things no longer needed, and the sense of purpose that had driven me to this place.

The stalemate was happening at approximately thirteen thousand feet on Quandary Peak, the thirteenth tallest mountain in Colorado, located approximately ten miles south of the skiing paradise of Breckenridge. It wasn't ski season, however. It was July, the height of the summer hiking and mountain climbing season in the Rockies. It's no secret that mountain climbing enthusiasts come from all over the country to climb the mountains of Colorado. Affectionately known as 14ers by those who climb them, there are fifty-three officially named and ranked mountains, and five named but unranked mountains, with summits above 14,000 feet in the state (14ers.com, 2015). In addition, there are 637 mountains in Colorado with peaks between 13,000-13,999 feet (13ers.com, 2015). The central and western parts of the state are a mountain climbing mecca for beginners, experienced technical climbers, and those with every skill level in between.

Those mountains were on my mind while slowly covering the miles of road between Alabama and Colorado in the moving truck, and I settled on a nice round number I would need to climb in order to feel both physically and mentally prepared to climb Kilimanjaro. Since arriving in Colorado in late April, Quandary Peak was the tenth 14er I was seeking to summit as part of my self-prescribed training regimen. Once I stood on the summit of this mountain, I could deem myself ready for Africa.

Climbing season began for me shortly after arriving in Colorado, building to a 14er attempt from short acclimatization hikes at elevations between 6,000 feet and 9,000 feet. Pikes Peak was the initial target. From the moment we arrived in Colorado Springs, I had surveilled Pikes. I went about the business of establishing a new residence while keeping a close eye on the peak from differing vantage points. The mountain I had first seen as a teen and had dreamt about for nearly three decades was right there, no matter where I was in the city, calling to me.

Two weeks after our arrival in Colorado, Eli and I set out on our second attempt to summit Pikes Peak. It was an exceedingly long, grueling day yet beautiful in many ways. Both of us had made much personal progress since our first attempt just six months earlier. However, at an elevation of just more than 12,000 feet, the Parkinson's symptoms slowed our progress significantly and eventually my legs could carry me no farther up the mountain. We had to make the tough decision to turn around and hike more than ten miles down the Barr Trail in order to make it back to the trailhead by sunset. Although we had fallen short of the summit yet again, it didn't feel like failure. It was another day spent together in the wilderness, and a valuable baseline measurement of the effort that would be required to reach the summit of Kilimanjaro.

On Quandary, the sky above the mountain was the deepest blue and the clouds slowly migrating eastward were the whitest of white as I continued to stare into the eyes of the mother mountain goat. An uneasy calm had settled over the standoff, and I lost track of time. How long had we been standing still, locked in each other's gaze? Ten minutes? Twenty minutes? It no longer mattered. I was beginning to understand that, just as had occurred several times on other mountains I had climbed over the course of the summer, our meeting was predetermined. God was teaching me something. I needed to pay attention and not carelessly let the moment pass by.

In one way, I was facing off against an odd reflection of myself. Like her, I was fearless when it came to protecting my children, willing to do whatever was necessary. The last patchy remnants of her outer coat were symbolic of my yet to be completed transformation into the person I was meant to be. Her unwavering instincts and spirit had brought her to this point, just as mine had done.

Mountain climbing is not all fun and games. In fact, there is much more suffering than one might imagine and, through the difficulties, one learns that mental endurance is more difficult to cultivate than physical endurance. With each step up that's ten times harder than one step down, one might ask, "Why am I doing this?" It was the question that Max had asked several times just a few weeks earlier.

While he was home on leave, Max and I set out to climb a couple of 14ers in one day. They would be his first two, and my seventh and eighth toward my goal of ten. Grays Peak and Torreys Peak are often climbed as a pair, especially since they share a common trailhead and the effort required is less than climbing them individually (going from peak to peak over a saddle between them before descending shortens the total distance hiked). He relished the idea of climbing mountains while home on leave, even more so because it was his first visit to Colorado after our move and since he was a toddler. After allowing a few days to begin acclimatizing to the significant increase in elevation from sea level at Camp Lejeune, it was time.

Once out on the trail, however, his tune changed. Max is not a morning person, and even less so when awakened at two a.m. for the three-hour drive to the trailhead, some of it over extremely rough road that required the use of four-wheel drive. He asked several times why we were doing this, grumbling mostly to himself that he could be at home fast asleep in a warm bed or eating a hearty breakfast instead of a carb bar with the texture and flavor of pavement. As the sun rose and the last remnant of darkness was replaced by the deep blue of the Colorado sky at high altitude, he began to appreciate how far we had come as he looked down over the valley we had traversed and at the mountains beyond.

As we neared the summit of Grays Peak his excitement grew, as if it was something he could no longer contain. After several minutes at the summit, posing for photos together, talking with others who were there, and just staring into the distance from more than fourteen thousand feet, Max turned to me and said, "I understand now." The struggle to reach the summit, which was much more mental than physical for a nineteen-year-old Marine, had been forgotten, replaced by the feeling of accomplishment at reaching a place that relatively few seek out, as well as the opportunity to see our world from such a unique vantage point.

After reaching the summit, Max understood that the struggle of the climb was just as valuable as the view from the mountaintop. It was an opportunity to grow and be changed, and it was something that couldn't be understood through someone else's eyes. It was something that had to be experienced. I believe that's why, when asked repeatedly about enduring such hardship and why he felt driven to climb Mt. Everest, George Mallory responded simply, "Because it's there."

Eli understood, too. A few weeks before Max came home on leave, Eli and I had taken on the challenge of climbing four 14ers in one day. Known as the Decalibron, the four mountains are Mt. Democrat, Mt. Cameron, Mt. Lincoln, and Mt. Bross. The repeated ascents and descents wore down our bodies to exhaustion, but the accomplishment was even sweeter after our failed attempts to climb Pikes. Four mountaintops in a single day moved us both countless miles down the road toward our goals.

There had been many moments when I wondered if I had made the right choice to cast aside all we knew and what little security had been reclaimed after the destruction of my former life and self. Sometimes, I had wondered if I was indeed as crazy as several friends and acquaintances had thought I was to sell nearly everything we owned to come to Colorado to train on the mountains. But with each mountain and each experience with my sons and others I had met along the way or at the summits, I became more certain this was the path I was meant to follow. None of them had been a clearer trail marker than the experience at the summit of my first 14er.

After the second attempt on Pikes Peak without reaching the summit, I shifted gears, needing some measure of success to propel me forward toward the goal. There are fifty-two other official 14ers in Colorado. All I had to do was pick one and go for it without the extra baggage that came with three decades of dreaming about reaching its summit. After some brief research on a website devoted to climbing the 14ers, I settled on Mt. Bierstadt to become what I hoped would be my first 14er summited.

Mt. Bierstadt is one of, if not the, most climbed mountains in Colorado. It is known as one of the easier 14ers, which is a purely relative comparison as none of the 14ers are easy. Its breathtaking beauty, proximity to Denver, ease of access with paved roads all the way to the trailhead, and a long, flat portion of trail through alpine marshland, all contribute to its popularity. Those attributes, combined with an early climbing season weekend, made for a packed trailhead parking lot well before daybreak. I squeezed into one of the last parking spots, grabbed my gear, and took care of a few necessities before turning on my headlamp and heading off into the predawn darkness. I felt good. Five weeks in Colorado had been long enough to acclimate to the change in altitude, overcome the stress of a cross-country move, and allow for the associated uptick in Parkinson's symptoms to subside. I liked my chances of success.

The brief explosion of yellow, orange, pink, and red above the summit as daybreak announced its arrival was spectacular and seemed to lessen gravity and pull me up the mountain, as if my legs weren't involved in the ascent at all. Just as quickly, the colors shifted and morphed into the blue daytime sky. Looking back on the path I had traveled and beyond, I began to understand why Pikes and her sister mountains pulled at something inside me, even though it is difficult to this day to adequately articulate it. Quite simply, it's just where I'm supposed to be. Nearly four hours after leaving the trailhead, my heart was pounding both from the thin air and my excitement as I made the final scramble up and over the large rocks leading to the summit.

As I reached the top of the mountain, I sought out the official United States Geological Survey elevation marker, which is typically embedded in stone at the summit. A man close to my age was taking a photo of the summit marker as I approached. I congratulated him on making it to the summit and we exchanged a high five. He beamed with pride, then just as quickly his expression changed. He smiled a smile that was on the verge of tears, then blurted out the first words I had expected to *think* upon reaching the summit, but the last words I expected to *hear,* "I have Parkinson's and I just climbed my first 14er!"

I was stunned, yet deep down not at all truly surprised, because this was yet another example of how God works in our lives. After a brief moment to recover, I smiled, introduced myself and said, "Do I have a story for you." I asked him to sit so we could talk. When I shared the relevant parts of my story and the quest for Kilimanjaro, it was his turn to be shocked. His name was Mark, and he had traveled to Colorado from Michigan to see his daughter and son-in-law. He was a key member of a local Parkinson's support group in his town, and sought to climb a 14er to show others in his group what was possible for them.

That two men with Parkinson's had traveled to Colorado from different parts of the country, compelled to climb the same mountain on the same day and reach the summit within minutes of each other, wasn't coincidence. It was a Divine appointment. Our meeting served to answer questions that we both had. Were we on the right path? Were we doing what God had set before us to accomplish? As we shared more of our life stories, our battles with Parkinson's, and what it meant to be having this conversation on the summit, we noticed that several others who had reached the summit were gathered around us listening and, like us, were enjoying what was transpiring at more than 14,000 feet.

A week after meeting Mark at the summit of Mt. Bierstadt, I finally made it to the summit of Pikes Peak on my third attempt. Armed with the newfound surety of being on the path meant for me, it didn't matter that the peak was enveloped in cloud cover as a summer storm rained down lightning on it. I finally conquered the mountain that had been such a part of my consciousness for decades. Reaching the summit of Pikes was special. Since that day I am able to look at the mountain that dominates the place I now call home and know that I once stood on top of it. Likewise, whenever I visit Denver I can look to the west at one of the most prominent mountains visible from the city, Mt. Evans, and know that I conquered it, as well.

On Quandary, the standoff with the mother goat came to an end as climbers who had already reached the summit and were on their way down the mountain came upon us. Surrounded and outnumbered by humans, the mother goat retreated over the steep side of the trail where we could not follow. Without hesitation, the kid followed the mother, and only then did the mountain goat who had been standing watch disappear over the ledge. My fellow climbers and I smiled and waved as we passed each other on the trail. They didn't know how long the standoff they briefly witnessed had been going on, and there was no need for them to know. I was relieved to finally be able move on toward my goal, although I was strangely sad that the intimate wilderness encounter had come to an end.

I reached the summit of Quandary Peak that day, fulfilling my training goal a full month before the scheduled departure date for Africa. I stayed on the peak for a long time, swapping mountain stories with other climbers and just enjoying the accomplishment and the view until an afternoon storm coming from the west warned that it was time to descend.

As the remaining weeks passed, I focused on final preparations. Sorting through gear and making a final push to meet my fundraising goal took most of my time. But I couldn't stay away from the mountains. I stole away to climb one more, and met a group of 30-somethings on Mt. Sherman that I remain in contact with to this day. And just days before leaving for Tanzania, I set out to reach the highest point in Colorado, Mt. Elbert.

It was at the summit of Mt. Elbert where I encountered a group of men and women who were celebrating heartily despite the sleet/snow mixture pelting us. An obviously fit woman stood and raised a beer in a toast. She had defeated cancer. After undergoing treatment and recovery, she and others in her group had traveled to the area for a mountain race to be held the next day. Not coincidentally, they came prepared to climb the tallest mountain in Colorado to celebrate as she declared her victory over cancer in the company of her husband and closest friends. Just as others had gathered around two guys with Parkinson's on the first summit I reached, I joined with them. It was fitting that I had the chance to witness another's victory declaration and celebration on the final mountain summit of my training.

I've often wondered what drives mankind to willingly endure the elements and extreme hardship to reach the summits of the world's tallest mountains. Is it a quest to go to the highest places where we can reach out to God and get a glimpse of His Glory? Is the mountaintop the best place to declare victory over our demons and enemies? I have looked deep inside myself for the answer, and have found that it is a mixture of both combined with an insatiable, innate curiosity to know what I am made of. I know I am ready for Kilimanjaro.

40

KILIMANJARO: DAY 5 - THE FINAL ASCENT

28 AUG 2012

If one were to strip away the arctic beanie and the shemagh wrapped tightly around my head, neck, and face, he or she would have unearthed a smirk. I could feel the expression on my face buried beneath its covering, held in place partly as a result of my somewhat sarcastic nature, but mostly because of the way Parkinson's contorts my facial muscles when I am under its attack. For months I had anticipated what my thoughts would be as I began the final assault on the mountain, yet the only thing that had been on my mind since we left high camp less than an hour before was that I was simply glad to be moving again, to be fighting off the cold that had nearly overwhelmed me. That was it. That was my grand thought as we settled into the rhythm of the climb.

Apart from the beautiful sunset view of Mawenzi and the sea of clouds beyond, the lodging experience at Barafu Camp had been one of the least rewarding of my entire life.

Everyone in the group was depleted when we reached high camp. No one wanted to eat, yet we force-fed ourselves in a sad attempt to replenish our energy stores in preparation for the night ahead. Although everyone looked worse for wear and had some small measure of doubt about each of our chances to reach the summit, we couldn't have known it would be the last time most of us would see one of our teammates.

I found it quite ironic that the coldest I had ever felt was a mere two-hundred miles south of the equator in Africa. It was the kind of cold that permeates every cell in the body, penetrating and eventually taking up residence in the marrow of bones. I'd been in the cold before, from the winds of winter that swept over north Texas for months on end to the desert cold of Utah and New Mexico to the mountain cold of Colorado, but this was different. This cold saturated me completely. Like all of the others, my tent was pitched on volcanic earth. There was little to no protection from the wind and cold outside, or from the chill emanating from the lonely rock beneath it. No matter what I tried in the attempt to get warm, the cold moved through my body as if ice had been injected into my veins.

Sleep? No, there had been no meaningful sleep during those few hours of allotted rest time. As desperate as I was for it to be merciful, sleep teased and mocked me, staying just beyond my grasp. With each passing moment without it, my monster gained strength and asserted itself, letting me know it would be loud and proud throughout the night ahead. Not only would the thin air and severe lack of essential oxygen conspire to trick my mind and body into believing that gravity had increased tenfold, my legs would also be slowed even more by the nearly frozen, slow-motion transfer of signals originating in my brain and passed on to muscles over a dopamine-depleted highway. Would the vessel that carries my soul commit the ultimate betrayal at the most crucial moment? I would know the answer before I saw my next sunrise.

After the guides had shaken the tents—not so subtly alerting us that "go time" was at hand—it had taken thirty minutes for the members of our group to make nearly frozen limbs perform their duties, wriggle free of tents, check backpacks, and test gear for readiness. One by one we deemed ourselves as ready as we could be for the night ahead and assembled in a tight group, moving our arms and stomping our feet to get the blood moving. Only then did we learn that our number would be reduced by one because of illness. At some point during the few hours of rest, Bella made the decision to end her pursuit of the summit. The nausea that had been her relentless companion since the second night at Shira Camp had taken the last bit of her strength, and she needed to sleep more than anything. She shared this with her friend and tent mate, and Kate conveyed to us Bella's well wishes for a good climb as we left Barafu Camp.

The initial hour or so of the climb out of high camp was fairly steep, enough so to warm the blood and chase away the cold from bones. The upward movement cleared the way for thoughts other than those focused solely on how not to be cold any longer. Oddly, the nighttime ascent reminded me of being a kid, stuck in the back seat of my parents' car, settling in for hours of sameness as we drove across the barren, flat parts of Texas and Oklahoma on routine trips to see extended family. To entertain myself and avoid the annoying presence of my younger brothers, I would study the bug splats on the windshield, drawing comparisons to real world things from the ornate remains of their carcasses on the glass. On this night, I was fascinated by the moon and the eerie yet beautiful glow it casts over the landscape. With several hours yet to go, it distracted me from the sameness of the darkness.

Nearly full, the moon dominated the sky. It seemed twice its normal size, as if it was stationed at the boundary of earth's atmosphere instead of a quarter million miles away. It hung just over my left shoulder in the outermost reaches of my peripheral vision. I had never before seen it consume so much of the night sky, and haven't since. Studying the moon entertained my mind as my body slowly dragged itself up the mountain. We parted ways with it as our group reached the top of the initial, steep leg of the climb and turned in a counterclockwise direction around the mountain on a fairly flat leg of the trek. The moon continued its routine and appointed trip to the west, and although I could no longer see it, the echoes of its light remained for a while longer before the contours of the mountain eventually blocked it from lighting our path altogether.

There was no sound other than the muffled, shuffling steps on the volcanic earth beneath our feet. As if a prison chain gang barred from talking by their overlords, we moved in unison, silently and in slow-motion with our heads down, mesmerized by the small piece of earth lit by headlamps. We tried to stay within arm's length of one another, reaching out periodically to steady the one in front of us as he or she began veering off the path, falling asleep while moving. I wondered if my younger, healthier teammates understood that so much of what they were experiencing was what it is like to live with Parkinson's.

At the end of the mild, counterclockwise traverse around the mountain, the trail took a hard left turn upward onto the small ridge we had just passed under, doubling back on the direction from which we had come. It was at this point, somewhere between sixteen and seventeen thousand feet, that the wheels started to come off. Dizziness overwhelmed me and the world swam in nauseating circles, much like the nights of college students when too much whiskey sets the world spinning out of control.

"Oh, no! Not like this, *not like this!*" The words screamed through my mind in a panic. I had sacrificed so much, had overcome so much, had hoped so much. Would it all come to an end as a casualty of altitude sickness? I was determined to not stop, each step becoming more difficult than the one before, all the while hoping that no one around me could see my struggle. I had no energy to argue with the guides should they choose to make me descend for my own good. In a last ditch effort to stay on the climb, I would willingly blame my discomfort on Parkinson's if asked, using it as a shield instead of an excuse. I would not surrender. I thought I would die trying, or more likely, pass out and fall flat on my face before I would voluntarily quit this quest. My entire worldview shrank and the whole of my being was funneled into just taking the next step.

At this point in the climb, it seemed as though we could go no farther than twenty-five yards at a stretch before needing to stop to rest and to ensure that we were hydrating properly. I don't know if they lasted two minutes or ten, but the breaks were never long enough. Each time, I leaned against or sat on a rock hoping that the dizziness would subside and the world would stop spinning. I might have prayed or slept for a moment or two during the breaks, but I'm unsure. The cycle of short gains and intermittent stops went on for hours. Or was it mere minutes? Time had taken on a distorted shape, and the ability to measure it had receded to some inaccessible part of my brain. I'm not sure at what point I entered into something akin to a dissociative fugue state. My memories of the next few hours are like the split-second snapshots one sees in a dark room lit only by a strobe light. While my body continued onward up the mountain, my mind sought refuge within its own elaborate constructs. As some of my teammates shared with me later, I wasn't the only one.

As their bodies focused on finding and making it to the next rock or landmark at the farthest reaches of their sight, and repeating the process over and over again, in the depths of their minds, Noah and Grace drew strength from and supported each other as they thought of their dad and his struggle.

Tyler fell into the warmth of time spent with family and loved ones celebrating happy occasions as he, too, focused on the next rock or point where a few moments of rest awaited. Of all of us, he seemed the most able to maintain mindfulness and focus on the task at hand.

As Dan labored for each breath, he reflected back on the multiple marathons he had run while relying on his physical abilities more so than extensive training. He felt the cough he had been hiding from others and the thin air on the mountain draining his sense of invincibility as if his veins had been opened up allowing his blood to flow freely onto the ground.

Near the back of the line, Brad kept it simple, allowing his mind to go wherever it wanted. He thought about his young family, and then about his friend fighting ALS. He knew just how fortunate he was to be here in the dark struggling for breath and inching his way to the summit. A tall man, he bumped his head on an overhanging rock along the trail, parting with a piece of his scalp. The blood and the pain brought him briefly back into the here and now, then the cold served to stop the bleeding and dull the pain, and the relentless climb once again separated his mind from his body.

With every step she took, Alex imagined she was walking beside her brother. Unable to walk on his own since the motorcycle accident and the resulting traumatic brain injury a year prior, Alex imagined that the strength leaving her body through the effort was being transferred to him, helping him to walk again. It was that sense of connection to her brother, her family, her loved ones, and humanity in general (in addition to her youth and vigor) that propelled her body to take the next step, then the next.

Adrift in the darkness with no sense of time or progress, Helen wondered if she had just started the climb or if she was near the summit. Feeling lost and disheartened, she drifted into and out of the here and now, disgruntled whenever Nick jarred her awake while still moving. They questioned if this hardship had been the best idea, the best way to celebrate the first anniversary of their union. Through the struggle, their bond became stronger. Even in the midst of their exhaustion and physical misery, they each counted on the other to stay tethered to the moment and the goal before them.

The cold was so painful that Annie's mind tried to detach from its grip, but wondered of she was losing the battle when the cold took on form and manifested as a blue woman floating beside her. Not good. There was danger in the darkness that wouldn't end. Both the cold and the unseen threat hunted her, but it did not dim her belief that failure wasn't an option. She hallucinated at times and fell asleep while walking, but the numbers propped her up. She counted—ten steps, or five sips of water, or three deep breaths of the thin air. Methodical and determined, her mind resorted to its most basic workings, its strength. It moved her slowly up the mountain toward a summit she was sure she would reach, but unsure if she would be able to see as the darkness threatened to consume any hope of sunrise.

The rocks became turtles and crawled away in Drew's mind, and every step he took upward moved the abyss behind him a step closer. Alone in the dark on the side of this cold mountain in Africa, he felt he had no choice but to go forward. If he faltered, where would he go? Into the abyss? Annie was still going, her small frame buried beneath layers of clothing. Drew knew all about her outsized determination, though, and he couldn't fall short in the competition with his future wife. It felt so real, the discomfort of knowing that she had made it and he hadn't. But, he knew it wasn't real, that he was still in the fight. The presence of the void behind him and the desire to not let Annie or himself down served to lift his right foot then his left in a seemingly never-ending cycle.

The very high altitude served as a hallucinogen that muddled the line between truth and fiction in Ava's mind, shaking her confidence to the core, leaving her with emptiness, exhaustion, and doubt. Ava's rocks didn't grow legs and move away like Drew's, but she did see the faces of various animals on some and the bored expression of the Mona Lisa on another. At one point, her shadow—arms extended while holding trekking poles—became a running man stick figure with a woman's voice. Yet, she kept moving, driven by an understandably fiery desire to never admit defeat combined with the warmth of the love and wonder she shared with her young niece. Before leaving for Africa, Ava had shown her Kilimanjaro's location on the relief globe in her room, and watched as the child's finger ran over the bump that represented the monstrous mountain she was now struggling to climb.

In a state somewhere between sleep and wakefulness, exhausted, overcome with nausea, and weakened by insufficient nutrition, Lizzie struggled to lift her head to focus on what she knew was the here and now. The brilliant points originating light years away captivated her, and the line of headlamps ahead danced like fireflies in a chorus line going up the mountain and meeting the stars in the sky. Then she was back on the climb. As her body staggered ever so slowly up the mountain, her mind then drifted back to the gym, repeating over and over again the number of steps required to climb the tallest manmade structure in the world, the Burj Khalifa. Hers was a constant fixture as the top-ranked name on the step machines, having climbed more than anyone else in the gym. Like a pro player knew how to close his eyes and make a basket from anywhere on the court, Lizzie's legs knew how to climb. The hours and hours of repetition had ensured it would be so.

As my body fought to overcome the incessant swirling of the dark world about me and to keep putting one foot in front of the other, my mind had taken me back to Pikes on the first day that Eli and I had attempted to reach its peak. We were in the clearing where he had found his demarcation line between war and peace, but we were no longer alone. We were accompanied by dozens if not hundreds of faceless others, each of them pushing me upward, saying, "I am you." I couldn't let them down, all those others who share the same enemy and the same fight. Here on this night on this mountain, the tallest of its kind in the world, I represented all those with Parkinson's and their hope to defeat the disease. I couldn't fail them or myself or all those who believed that I could do this, but the fight was hard.

After the summer spent training in the Rockies, I knew how my body felt from the effects of high altitude. The many years prior had taught me how it feels for Parkinson's to restrain my body's response to the signals emanating from my brain. Learning to distinguish between the two wasn't easy as the manifestations are so similar. Rather than one or the other, I felt as though I was outnumbered two to one and fighting both while on the steep incline. I wasn't convinced that the desire to not let those down who were rooting for me would be enough to drive me to the summit.

As the night and the climb progressed, our ragged group continued ever so slowly up the unrelenting switchbacks in the darkness. We were together, yet each of us was locked away in a world deep inside our minds. Mine took me from the mountains of Colorado to the heat and humidity of Parris Island, where my sons had become men and Marines over thirteen weeks of training. How could I give in to the suffering of one night and fail to reach the summit when my children had endured day after day and night after night of rigorous training, culminating in the days-on-end test of their mettle known as the Crucible? How could I not continue to make my brain make my legs move up this mountain when Eli had taken countless steps in Afghanistan while not knowing if each one would be his last? These two men who I love and respect more than any others demanded that I not give up and overcome the enemy once and for all. I held tightly to that thought as I took the next step then the next. I could not let them down.

41

KILIMANJARO: DAY 5 - UHURU PEAK

28 AUG 2012

The separation between heaven and earth was razor thin. It burst into existence as a bright orange, horizontal line that appeared to have no beginning or end. Even at this early stage after its birth, it heralded something so familiar yet so unlike anything we had ever seen. Growing incrementally in breadth with each passing second, the sunrise seen from 18,000 feet was the magical antidote that pulled each of us from the madness in the darkness that had threatened to consume us throughout the night.

As if waking from a bad dream, I was suddenly aware of my surroundings and my own existence. I stopped and sat, facing east. The sky above the orange line grew lighter before the ground beneath it, slowly allowing the shapes of the mountain below and the sea of clouds extending to the horizon to be seen. In a flash of total lucidity, I tried to absorb the sight, aware that for me the moment had not come before and may never come again. How many people had seen a sunrise at

243

this height while still touching the earth? The opportunity to do so added to my definition of riches. Being here in this moment was priceless. It is one of the few times in life that I have experienced true wonder and awe, surpassed only by the moment I was born of the Spirit, when my wife said yes, and when our sons entered this world.

I savored the moment for as long as possible before being urged to stand and press on. Our original goal had been to experience this at the summit and, obviously, we had not achieved it. We were more than two hours and thirteen-hundred vertical feet behind schedule as we struggled against the steepness of the incline and the loose scree that cut each torturous step by half in effectiveness. Without the darkness to band us together so tightly, the group spread out as each moved according to his or her own pace, similar to an Olympic 5,000-meter race if one were to watch it in extra super slow-motion. Progress was excruciatingly slow, and made even slower by the need to stop and rest briefly every ten to twenty yards. Not only was I at the back of the pack, but also I was slowly falling farther and farther behind.

I had been in similar positions over the previous summer, looking up at a steep incline toward a summit just out of my sight, and had found a way to reach it. But I had also been close on Pikes, the mountain that had held residence in my mind for years, and had failed to make it multiple times before eventually succeeding. I had experienced both success and failure, and I really didn't know which it would be today.

Parkinson's was crushing me from all sides as if I was in a pressure chamber. Throughout the night, I had broken through barrier after barrier to keep going when I didn't know if I could. But, now, each step felt as though it was the last possible measure of effort and energy I had to spend. I wondered if all the others fighting Parkinson's, who knew about and supported the climb, would understand if I fell short of reaching the summit. Would my friends know that their prayers and positive thoughts had helped me to go as far as my body and mind could? That key part of my being that wants nothing more than for my family to be proud of me yearned to know if they would be okay with my failure. Would they understand that I had given my all? Would they still love and respect me?

"Papa, tell me the story about The Mountain," a child's voice echoed in the recesses of my mind. I wasn't hallucinating (was I?), because I could savor the warmth of the sun at high altitude, because I could still see my teammates up ahead, and because I could see a beautiful glacier, only a fragment of the ice cap that once covered Kilimanjaro, above and to the left of me. It wasn't my sons' voices I had heard, and they had always called me Dad, anyway. The voice wasn't one from the past, but rather one from the future.

"Papa, tell me the story about The Mountain." It was my grandchild's voice, but I had no grandchildren, yet. Like any parent of adult children, I had thought of what it would be like to be a grandparent someday, but I had never thought of it with such clarity. The idea, the voice, came from an unfamiliar place in my mind or soul, yet it knew how I yearned to be called Papa.

"Papa, show me the mountaintop picture," the sweet little voice said. Now, fully in the moment yet lived, I pulled the photo from my wallet and held it between my thumb and forefinger, rubbing the tattered edges. Taking the photo from my hand, the child exclaimed excitedly, *"That's you on top of The Mountain!"* The little one stared intently at the photo of me,

standing in front of the big green sign, then said, *"I want to be like you, Papa. Someday, I'll stand on The Mountain, too."*

Then, just like that, the time machine in my mind brought me back from the future and deposited me just feet from the crater rim. Having little to no memory of how I reached this point in the climb, I was confused at first. As if the volume of my hearing was slowly being turned up, I heard the voices of my teammates saying, "You're almost there!" and then I saw a big, ugly, green sign. Was I at the summit? No, not yet, but close. After enduring a hug, a few high fives, and a slap on the back, I looked at the sign that read, "Congratulations! You are now at Stella Point. ALT 5,739M A.M.S.L. Tanzania." Only a slow march around the crater rim remained. When I had had nothing left, my child's child yet conceived had shown me the way up the toughest part of the climb. Someday, when my grandchild stands on top of The Mountain, he or she will likely feel a sense of *déjà vu* and think of me.

From Stella Point, if I squinted and focused with the few remaining brain cells still alive and awake in my skull, I could see Uhuru Peak in the distance up and around the crater rim. We had made it this far, though, and all doubt was gone. I believed that no matter how battered and exhausted we felt, we would make it to Uhuru Peak. If one fell down, the others would dig deep and find the strength to carry him or her to the summit. After a long break and with one more *Twende?* serving as the start to the race, we were off again in extra super slow-motion up and around the crater rim.

It seemed a bit odd after the long night of madness to be fully cognizant of the experience at very high altitude. Perhaps it was a massive shot of adrenaline coursing through my body that enabled my brain to function at a higher level than it had for several hours. I remember how I felt and what I saw during the slow march on the crater rim. As I looked to my left, I was mesmerized by and fascinated with being so close to an actual glacier, not to mention that it was within the same week I had trekked through a rain forest. I looked to my right at Kilimanjaro's most evident crater, imagining the spectacle and violence of the volcanic eruptions that had burst forth from the African plains hundreds of thousands of years before it was known as Africa.

A few steps behind me, Dan was bringing up the rear of the pack on this last leg of the climb, his lungs, already weakened from the cough that had harassed him for weeks on end, struggling now to take in enough air to power his steps. Just ahead of him, Brad walked by my side. Neither of us said more than a word or two as we inched closer to the summit. Then I saw it. After clearing a rock outcropping on the right side of the path, beyond a slight dogleg to the right and up, the summit was in clear view and I could see my teammates just below the sign. Brad took a few steps back and away from me, motioning for me to go on alone in the company of my thoughts and emotions.

Those emotions were welling up inside, overriding conscious thought, as I reached the gauntlet of teammates, each one taking the time to share in my victory with hugs and congratulations and making way for me to go to the sign by myself. The big green sign with its stickers and plastic lines of prayer flags flapping in the wind at its base and the deep blue sky surrounding it was like a magnet for my soul. It pulled me to it, helpless to resist. The moment I touched the sign, I yelled something incoherent, something loud and guttural from the depths of my soul. My grip tightened and I shook the sign so hard I thought I had broken it after the initial moment of triumph passed.

It had taken nearly a decade and a lot of suffering, sacrifice, dedication, countless miles of training, the immeasurable love of family and friends, and the Grace of God to make it from Parkinson's diagnosis to the summit of Mt. Kilimanjaro. On the morning of 28 August 2012, I reached freedom and stood where no one imagined I could be on the day I had been given a life sentence. Touching the sign at the top of Africa meant that I had finally conquered Parkinson's. No matter what it had taken or ever will take from me during the course of the battle, it was the moment that I knew with certainty that it will never, ever win.

42

KILIMANJARO:
DAY 6 - THE WAY DOWN

29 AUG 2012

The Tanzanians gathered in a group preparing for our send off. The guides, porters, cooks and other support personnel were happy with the successful completion of the climb and another week of work, but more so with their pockets full of shillings from the customary tips given by climbing groups on the last morning on the mountain. They gathered with their backs to the peak, so far away now. It was still hard to believe that we had stood on it just twenty-four hours earlier. The view of the peak was spectacular from Mweka Camp, purposefully framed as a backdrop behind the Tanzanians for the making of personal videos and taking of photos.

A half day's hike through the rainforest to the Mweka Gate was all that remained between us and celebrating the completion of our climb. Although it had been an experience of a lifetime, we were all looking forward to leaving Kilimanjaro

National Park for our hotel in Arusha where hot showers, an assortment of good food, and, for some, an overabundance of alcoholic beverages awaited.

There were still some memories to be made in the park, though, and in this moment it would be the men who had taken great care of our group singing the customary Kilimanjaro song. They sang and clapped, and after a round through the verse, we joined with them, stumbling through the words but enjoying ourselves nonetheless.

> *Jambo! Jambo bwana!*
> Hello! Hello sir!
> *Habari gani? Mzuri sana!*
> How are you? Very well!
> *Wageni, mwakaribishwa!*
> Guests, you are welcome!
> *Kilimanjaro? Hakuna matata!*
> Kilimanjaro? No trouble!
> *Tembea pole pole. Hakuna matata!*
> Walk slowly, slowly. No trouble!
> *Utafika salama. Hakuna matata!*
> You'll get there safe. No trouble!
> *Kunywa maji mengi. Hakuna matata!*
> Drink plenty of water. No trouble!
> *Kilimanjaro, Kilimanjaro,*
> Kilimanjaro! Kilimanjaro!
> *Kilimanjaro, mlima mrefu sana.*
> Kilimanjaro, such a high mountain.

The trip down from Uhuru Peak to our current location had taken approximately nine hours, and it had been nearly as difficult on our bodies as the nighttime ascent. It was an utterly forgettable experience apart from some unforgettable hardships. It didn't take long for the high of the mountaintop experience to fade as the adrenaline rush subsided and exhaustion, hunger, and an unquenchable thirst dominated our existence as we stumbled down the loose scree like zombies. At various times, several members of the group just stopped in their tracks, waiting for a sip of water or a bite of candy or carb bar before their bodies and minds could break free from the inertia and continue on.

As was the case on the last part of the ascent, Dan and I lagged far behind the rest of the group, which was my fault. We wouldn't have been so far behind the others had I not been so reluctant to leave the summit. While everyone else in the group had been eager to descend, I had wanted to stay. It had taken so much commitment, sacrifice, effort, and time to reach the summit, and I didn't want it to be over so quickly. Two assistant guides stayed with us, finally urging us to begin our descent while watching us closely and carrying our packs after we reluctantly surrendered to their polite demands to do so. We stumbled into Barafu Camp nearly a full hour after the others, where we were the last to receive some disturbing news.

Will had been evacuated from the peak to the small medical treatment room at Mweka Camp because of dehydration and altitude sickness. When I last saw him, we were celebrating and taking group photos on the summit. In the midst of our personal celebrations, I had somehow missed that he had been whisked away. In addition, we learned that when Bella awoke around the same time we had reached the summit, she had developed a cough, which meant that her simple nausea had progressed into a case of troubling altitude sickness. She was quickly evacuated down the mountain to Mweka Camp for evaluation and treatment.

Since Dan and I had arrived much later than the others, the rest break at Barafu Camp was more brief than the pit stop had been the night before. It allowed only enough time to pack my duffel, repack my backpack, grab a quick bite of leftover snacks in the meal tent, and start walking down the mountain again. I was able to hang with the pace of the group, and the mood was light after the brief stop to rehydrate, subdue our hunger, and be still for just long enough to allow our brains and bodies to once again be on the same page.

When we arrived at Mweka Camp a few hours later, we were greeted by Will. He was doing much better after resting and receiving fluids, but still weak. He had been told that although Bella had responded well to treatment, before he had arrived she had been evacuated to a hospital in Moshi as an additional precaution and to continue the treatment for altitude sickness. We would stop in Moshi to pick up Bella on the way back to the hotel, and we would do our best to lift her spirits which would hopefully help her to feel better physically.

In the mean time, each of us needed food and desperately needed to crash inside our tents after the most physically and mentally demanding thirty-six hours of our lives. The slightly more than 4,000 feet of ascent to the summit the night before had been followed by more than 9,000 feet of knee-crushing descent during the day (Stedman, p. 328). To say we were physically broken would be an incredible understatement. No one had trouble falling or staying asleep during our last night on the mountain.

After the singing of the Kilimanjaro song and the exchange of handshakes and hugs among climbers and crew, we started the last leg of the descent through the rain forest. Wanting to forget the less than memorable descent of the day before, I was looking forward to a leisurely hike down through the warm, humid forest environment to shake off the last bit of freezing cold still reluctant to give up its hold on me. What we hadn't anticipated was the mud. Every step down through the forest was treacherous. I had expected a near mindless exercise to cap off the whole Kilimanjaro experience, but instead, it was a tension-filled exercise in concentration. Will and Steven had gone ahead of the group to the Mweka Gate to tend to the required administrative duties and prepare our certificates of completion prior to our arrival. Based on the slog through the mud, I couldn't see how they could make much better time than the rest of the group.

By the time our group arrived at the Mweka Gate, our boots were unrecognizable as such, totally encased in globs of rich Tanzanian earth. The porters for our group had established a small base near the gate, setting out folding chairs for us to sit, relax, and enjoy the completion of the climb. Having expended what remained of our energy on the descent through the rainforest, we gladly fell into them and accepted the drinks and snacks offered. Young boys took the boots right off our feet to clean them in exchange for tips, which felt like an absolute luxury at this point. We enjoyed the celebratory atmosphere at the gate for some time, while locals with handmade wares bartered with some from our group and other climbers temporarily stationed at the gate, hoping for one last sale or exchange of goods before we left the park.

We marveled at the wonderful job the young boys had done with our boots in such short order, each pair looking better than they had since they were new, and rewarded them handsomely for their work. Reluctantly, we struggled to pull ourselves from the comfort of the chairs and make the short walk to the bus for our departure. As the bus passed slowly through the gate, we were told by the driver that Will and Steven would meet us and board the bus just down the road.

As we left Kilimanjaro National Park for what was most likely the last time in our lives, the looks on our faces were ones of tired contentedness and our hearts were filled with a sense of completion. We had achieved our individual goals, and were now able to look back on what had transpired, relishing the experience of a lifetime. The last thing any of us expected was that although our trip down the mountain was complete, our descent was not. We were about to discover just how much further it could go. If the telling of the story was fiction, ending it with reaching the summit of Kilimanjaro and the celebration upon completion of the climb would have been the perfect ending. Unfortunately, real life can be messy and brutal, and triumph can be accompanied by tragedy.

43

TRIUMPH AND TRAGEDY

A great soul never dies.
It brings us together again and again.

MAYA ANGELOU

She was gone. Just like that. The kind, smart, happy, adventurous, adorable young woman—our teammate— was gone.

As soon as Will and Steven boarded the bus, it was evident that something was terribly wrong. The skin around Will's eyes was the shade of red typically left in the wake of tears, and he was visibly shaking. Steven, standing behind Will for support, was unusually stern and his face bore much sadness, a look that needed no translation. With what seemed like the last bit of breath he could muster, Will informed us that Bella had unexpectedly passed away the evening before at a hospital in Moshi. As the words left his mouth, a shockwave of despair spread throughout the small bus, resulting in loud gasps, words of disbelief, and anger that such a horrible event had occurred. We had just been to the top of Africa, and now it felt like we were free-falling into the deepest, darkest pit in all the land.

After the initial shock subsided, the questions followed. A few of my team members asked again and again how something like this could have happened. Others fought through angry tears, wanting details like whether there were signs or who was with her at the hospital. And some were silent. I was thinking, *Not again.* On fifteen separate occasions during Eli's Afghanistan deployment, I learned of the death of a vibrant, exceptional young man. Each time I mourned, and each time I had asked God what good, what purpose was fulfilled with the loss of the young. And each time I had received no answer, not that I had expected one, and I knew that no answers would be found in this lifetime. Now, it was my teammate who was dead. Although she was someone I knew only briefly, a bond had been formed through a shared experience. It was the first time that I was grateful for the hard walk with Eli, the listening and trying to help him make sense of something as senseless as someone close to him dying.

As difficult as it was, we had to move forward. We couldn't sit on the side of the road in the bus forever, and we had to decide how to proceed. Will asked the group for input. Do we go to the hospital in Moshi and pay our respects to Bella, or do we go to the hotel? Overwhelmingly, the notion was to go to the hospital, although none of us had any idea what to expect. Had we known, I believe the decision would have been different. We wanted to do the right thing to honor our fallen friend and teammate, but in our shock and grief it was difficult to know what the "right thing" was.

The bus ride going away from Kilimanjaro was the polar opposite of the bus ride we had been on coming to the mountain. As we had approached the mountain, in what now seemed like a lifetime ago, the bus was filled with anticipation and excitement for the adventure to come. Now the ride to the hospital in Moshi was surreal, one filled with disbelief, despair, and an overwhelming sense of dread. When we arrived at the hospital, we were met with the stark reality that we weren't in America. Although we didn't see much of the best hospital in the area, it was a shock to see the disparity between it and the quality of the medical facilities we were accustomed to in the United States. It reminded me that many Americans have such little understanding regarding just how fortunate and blessed we truly are.

Steven and his assistant guides were kind and compassionate as they accompanied our group onto hospital grounds, leading the reluctant band of brothers and sisters into a place we really didn't want to be, toward an experience we really didn't want to have, yet felt compelled to live through anyway. I tried to ready myself by remembering what it had been like the night all those years ago when I had received the call from the VA hospital that my father was on death's door. By the time I arrived, he was gone. When I entered the room where his body lay, it was spartan. The tubes and wires had been removed, his face cleaned, his hair brushed, and his hands folded neatly over perfectly smoothed out bed sheets. He had looked more peaceful in death than I had ever seen him in life.

What we experienced in Moshi was far different from what I recalled of the day my father died. We were led to the morgue, where we were allowed to enter in pairs to pay our last respects. It was not a spartan environment, and no effort had been made to alter Bella's appearance from the frantic and rough environment in which the doctors and nurses had attempted to save her life. As we left the hospital morgue, I regretted that I would carry with me for some time this image of her, now intermingled with the memories of the big smile and bright eyes of the young woman I had known on the mountain. I believe that most of my teammates felt the same, although we have since avoided talking about the experience.

Later that evening, after bathing for the first time in a week and forcing down food we needed but didn't have the heart to enjoy, we met in a private meeting room at the hotel with an American grief counselor called in by the adventure travel company. We half-heartedly listened to her words, but none of them were assimilated in our minds. How could she know what we felt? She hadn't been there on the mountain. She wasn't Bella's friend or teammate. It must have been similar to what combat veterans feel like when sitting across from a civilian counselor at a VA medical center, trying to relate their combat experience to someone who had not a clue other than what he or she had learned in college.

We sat there for some time listening to the grief counselor ramble on and on, none of us willing to be the first to stand and simply walk out of the meeting. It felt like torture on top of torment. The only thing I specifically recall about the meeting was learning that the suspected cause of Bella's death was high altitude pulmonary edema, or HAPE. Essentially, it is a fluid buildup in the lungs, occurring in mostly healthy people capable of mountaineering, and is a major cause of death related to high-altitude trekking.

None of it made sense to me. Earlier in the year she had traveled to Peru to hike the Inca Trail to Machu Picchu, with much of the trek spent above 8,000 feet, the altitude above which most cases of HAPE occur. It's also a common marker above which most mountaineers know to be on the lookout for signs of altitude sickness. Based on her overtly happy description of that adventure, she had suffered no ill effects during the trip.

I am definitely not a physician, and I was frustrated by my lack of knowledge in regard to the nuances and complexities of high altitude medicine. We wanted answers. We wanted to know why our friend and teammate had died. Had she received proper treatment on the mountain and at the hospital? But it was slowly dawning on each of us that we would most likely never know the answers to our questions. We weren't her family and, therefore, had no right to seek specific answers via formal channels. Regardless of the questions we harbored, we were slowly coming to grips with the fact that Bella was gone and there was nothing we could do about it.

After the meeting, several members of the group had a decision to make regarding whether or not to go on safari, which was scheduled to begin the next morning. Roughly a third of the group was scheduled to depart for the States, and the remainder had committed to the after-climb Serengeti safari months ago, myself included. There was no solid ground to stand on or clear basis to make a decision, and there was no precedent. Stay or go?

My gut was telling me that I wasn't ready to go home yet. I needed time to think about, reconcile, and to try to make sense of the two opposing experiences: the long sought after victory and the unexpected tragedy. I didn't want to be around outsiders in that moment. I wanted to be close to my teammates and friends, to those who were struggling with the same thoughts and emotions I had. The last thing I needed was to be locked inside an airplane with hundreds of strangers for nearly twenty-four hours. I needed vast, open spaces to think and to sort through the swirling mess inside my head. I needed the African wilderness.

44

A SMALL MEASURE OF PEACE

"For my thoughts are not your thoughts,
neither are your ways my ways," declares the Lord.

Isaiah 55:8, ESV

I awoke at dawn on the last morning of the safari, not far from the site known as the "cradle of mankind." Considered to be one of the most significant sites in the world for the study of paleoanthropology, the Olduvai Gorge lay approximately fifteen miles to the northwest of our camp. We were perched on the western rim of the Ngorongoro Crater, the largest inactive volcanic caldera in the world. Created millions of years ago when a large volcano erupted then collapsed in on itself, the crater is a rich environment where tens of thousands of wild animals live in a protected world similar to what I imagine the Garden of Eden must have been like.

For the third night in a row, I had slept dreamlessly and deeply in the African wild. More than likely, the much needed rest resulted from a combination of my body recovering after the extreme demands that climbing Kilimanjaro had placed on it, and my mind going into shutdown mode after hours spent trying to make sense of everything that had occurred since arriving in Africa nearly two weeks prior. The first day of safari had been the toughest. Bella's death and the image of her in the morgue were still fresh in my mind. We had plenty of time to think about it as we bounced around inside the rugged safari vehicle on barely passable roads for more than eight hours as we made our way from Arusha to the heart of Serengeti National Park.

The safari turned out to be one of the few times in life that it was actually possible to run away from problems. Or at least it had felt like it. Now several days and a few hundred miles traveled after learning about the passing of our teammate, I was just beginning to reconcile three vastly different experiences: claiming a long-awaited and hard-earned victory on top of Kilimanjaro, the despair resulting from the death of our teammate, and the peace cultivated in the remote African wild where life and death happen every day.

I stood beneath an enormous, old Acacia tree in the center of the camp looking east as the sun rose over and revealed the massive crater. That I was able to marvel at what I saw and clearly appreciate the location where I stood was progress. After learning of Bella's passing, the victory and the tragedy were jumbled together and I was unable to separate the two. Over the past few days, however, my thoughts had slowly precipitated and settled into the realization that the events could indeed be separated. I could still relish the triumph while also mourning her loss. I also believed, from the brief time that I knew her, that she would want us to be able to celebrate reaching the summit.

I was able to arrive at this point in part by reflecting upon the lessons Eli had taught me about losing people close to him. He and the rest of his fellow Marines believe the best way to honor their fallen brothers is to never forget them and to honor them by living the best lives possible. I had spent several hours questioning God and wondering why He would take me from the scrap heap, a man broken and discarded by the world, then rebuild me to be able to conquer mountains, yet take from us someone so young and with so much to offer the world. It was during a stop in the middle of the Serengeti the day prior that I was able to find some measure of peace. As I stood in the knee-high grass in a vast expanse of the African plains under an even bigger blue sky, I lifted my hands in the air to God, surrendering my lack of understanding, relinquishing my need to know, and just being thankful to be alive.

45

FULL CIRCLE

"For I know the plans I have for you,"
declares the Lord,
"plans to prosper you and not to harm you,
plans to give you hope and a future."

JEREMIAH 29:11, NIV

Coming home had been much more difficult than I had imagined it would be. In fact, I hadn't imagined it would be difficult at all. Everything seemed different, though, and it wasn't just a case of delayed jet lag. It was like getting a new pair of glasses when I didn't know I needed them, then suddenly I can see the world around me much more clearly. Sometimes it's a good thing, and sometimes it's not. A full week had passed, yet I still felt disoriented.

For two weeks I had lived in a brutally simple world. I had become accustomed to sleeping in a tent at high altitude in harsh weather conditions and in the middle of the Serengeti with armed guards surrounding the encampment to watch for lions or stampeding elephants in the darkness. I had eaten less and less each day, grateful for whatever food was available, adjusting to smaller portions, and becoming acquainted with hunger as a frequent companion. I had focused on simple tasks, like channeling all of my concentrated effort into just taking the next step or reaching a landmark in the distance. I had seen the night sky in its purest form, free from the re-fracted, hazy glow of manmade light. My soul had welcomed the quiet, soothing sounds of nature, from the rhythm of the rainforest to the song of the mountain to the chorus of the African plains. I had lived in a small community of people with similar, unified goals and who were kind and shared a common, giving spirit. I was cared for by others who had few possessions but who were rich with contentment for the lives they had been given.

Returning home, I was disoriented by how fast everything moved, how noisy every environment seemed to be, how pol-luted the sky and the land appeared, how saturated by excess nearly every aspect of our daily lives are, how divided we are in purpose and direction, but mostly by the lack of commu-nity and how isolated we are even in the midst of mass hu-manity. Everything that had seemed so normal to me before I boarded the plane to Africa now seemed so foreign, as if my world had been knocked from its axis. Had the world changed so drastically while I had been away, or was it me who had changed? Even as I asked the question, I knew the answer. It was me. Definitely me. Strangely, I didn't want what I was feel-ing to fade. I didn't want to be fully reassimilated back into the noise. I wanted to hang onto feeling different, to seeing the world in a unique way, to appreciating the smallest of bless-ings. Without question, there was a part of me that wanted to hop on the next flight back to Tanzania and continue living a simple and extremely spiritual life.

I had been unusually quiet around Liv since I returned, sharing only the pleasant or humorous details of the safari, the climb, and the victory of reaching the summit of Kilimanjaro. Especially the victory. It was her triumph as much as mine. After all, without her love and compassion through the darkest of times, I wouldn't be alive, much less a victor. There were many people who shared in the victory, especially those who needed the hope of knowing that they, too, could accomplish the unimaginable in spite of, or even because of, their challenges. I looked forward to sharing the story of the road to the summit of Kilimanjaro with them, to lifting them up, to encouraging them to reach for and live out their dreams. But first, I would need to sort through all of my thoughts.

Apparently, I was in the process of doing just that while standing in front of the fridge, the doors held open by their handles in my hands. "Snap out of it," Liv yelled, while snapping her fingers in front of my face, her last ditch effort to get my attention after not receiving a reply to a question asked multiple times. "What are you doing?" she demanded, quizzically. I didn't know how long I had been staring into the confines of the fridge.

"Do you know how long I could survive just on the condiments alone in this fridge?" I asked, earnestly. She gave me the face palm gesture in response. "No, seriously, I could live for two or three weeks just by eating everything in this glorious box of goodness that we look past every time we open the door and complain that there's nothing to eat," I protested.

"You're so weird," she stated emphatically. Then she followed up her evaluation with a question and an additional observation, "Did you suffer brain damage over there or some-thing? You've been acting strangely ever since you returned." That's us, I thought. My brain is dying and she's making jokes about it. God, how I love this woman. I laughed. Yes, it was me that had changed. Definitely me.

"You need to get ready," she commanded while walking out of the room, "Eli will be here soon. His flight leaves in a few hours."

An hour later, Eli settled into the passenger seat for the ride north from the Springs to Denver International Airport. He would soon be on his way to Indiana for a memorial gath-ering with the family and friends of his mentor and brother Marine, Cpl. Bishop. It had been two years since he died in combat in Afghanistan, and although Eli looked forward to celebrating his life with those who loved Bishop, he was brac-ing himself for the reopening of wounds still struggling to heal. It had been Bishop's death that led Eli to make that fate-ful September call home, the call that had set so many things in motion over the last twenty-four months.

Through time spent together and the honing of my under-standing of his moods, I knew he had a lot on his mind and that he wanted to talk about his combat experiences, which was rare. Whenever he needed to talk, especially about the war, I knew to simply listen without asking questions. As we made our way north on I-25, he opened up about the loss of his friends and his personal struggles in learning to deal with his grief and the guilt he bore for surviving when his broth-ers hadn't. Then he recounted each experience he and I had shared since he returned from war. Together we had marched through the New Mexico desert with thousands of others, and hiked the mountains of Colorado and the trails leading to the famed arches near the Canyonlands of Utah. Slowly, with each new experience and the passage of time, he shared that he had learned that life can still be beautiful after traumatic events like combat and the deaths of people he loved.

"I'm finally back, dad," he said matter-of-factly. "This is as close to normal as I can be. I can't express how much I appreciate everything you and mom have done to help me. Watching your recovery and seeing all the things you've been able to do after so many years of struggle has taught me that anything is possible. And seeing the photo of you on top of Kilimanjaro," he struggled to get the words out now, "well, what I'm trying to say is that you guys helped save me."

When we arrived at the airport terminal, Eli grabbed his bag and we exchanged a bear hug and an "I love you" before parting ways. As I drove away, I watched him disappear into the terminal in my rearview mirror, and thought of the last time we had parted ways while going in opposite directions. How different from today that day was on the North Carolina coast when he had departed for war and my new life had been conceived. With Eli's words, everything had come full circle.

In a broad sense, God used Parkinson's disease to radically change and eventually save me. He trusted me with a new story for my life—a reclaimed life, a rebuilt life, a redeemed life—to bring Him glory, and to use the years of struggle and the unimaginable life that has followed to help and to serve others. God had given me hope, purpose, and direction.

Specifically, God used a father and a son to help save the other. He used my love for my son to motivate me, inspiring me to become who I was meant to be. He had given me the command to get up and walk so that I could meet my son where he needed me to be, to walk beside him in his struggle, to join forces with him to push the rock, to play a part in navigating through his storm.

This part of my mission fulfilled, I drove toward the Rockies, toward home. I didn't know what the future held, but the long, unlikely road to Kilimanjaro had taught me that anything is possible.

EPILOGUE

MARCH 2015

I will rejoice and be glad in your steadfast love,
because you have seen my affliction;
you have known the distress of my soul,
and you have not delivered me into the hand of the
enemy;
you have set my feet in a broad place.

PSALM 31:7-8, ESV

Her fine, sandy brown hair, pulled up in tiny pigtails, glistens in the afternoon sun as she skitters from one piece of playground equipment to another. First crawling through the plastic tunnel then climbing on objects low to the ground, she repeats the circuit over and over again. Only eighteen months old, she's gaining confidence in her petite body and the things it can do. When the time comes to leave the playground, she looks up at her mommy, pleading with her blue-gray eyes and saying, "More! More!" Her father, my son, swoops in and lifts her high in the air, and she smiles and giggles with glee.

Two and a half years have passed since I stood on the summit of Kilimanjaro, and the grandchild who lived only in my heart, the one who led me up the toughest part of the climb, is now a reality. Her mother is the love of her father's life and her existence is the evidence of second chances. They give Eli's life purpose and direction.

After raising two sons from boys to men and Marines, Liv is overjoyed with everything the little bundle of femininity brings into her life, relishing every detail of the moment, every little thing she does. I love being her Papa, playing hide and seek and watching her color with crayons when I'm with her, and in the times I'm not, daydreaming about all the wonderful things she will do and the lives she will touch. Will she climb mountains? Will she one day stand in the places I've been? Will she go further than I can possibly imagine?

When I returned from Africa, I had many thoughts, emotions, and questions to contend with. What did reaching the summit of Kilimanjaro really mean? Obviously, I was blessed with an extraordinary victory, experienced unexpected tragedy, made new friends and teammates for life, and was a part of a group who made a substantial contribution to Parkinson's research. But it was the deeper, internal changes that define the Kilimanjaro experience for me, and it serves as a blueprint for how to live the remainder of my life.

In the months that followed my return home, I sought the answers to my questions. When I stood on the summit, had I reached the pinnacle of great things I am to do in life? Why had God driven me to do it and why had it been so important? Why had I been successful when so many others aren't? What purpose did it serve? With every question, there was the seeking of my Creator and, ultimately, the expression of the basic human desire to know why I was created and for what purpose.

Again, I asked most of those same questions a little more than a year after I stood atop Kilimanjaro. Seven thousand six hundred miles from the summit, my lungs and legs ached much the same as they had on summit day, even though I was just mere feet above sea level with the full compliment of oxygen in the air surrounding me. Uhuru Peak represents freedom for Tanzania and its citizens, just as the metropolitan area where I stood on that beautiful October day represents freedom to the world.

Across the Potomac River from Washington, D.C., at the entrance to Arlington National Cemetery, stands the United States Marine Corps War Memorial. It depicts the raising of the American flag atop Mount Suribachi on Iwo Jima during World War II. After several months of rigorous, dedicated training, I stood at the base of the memorial while wearing a finisher's medal around my neck. Exhausted and battered by injuries, yet full of joy, I had run and finished the Marine Corps Marathon in honor of my sons.

Just a few months later, I sought the answers to the questions in the company of another Parkinson's warrior while crossing the Pyrenees mountain range on foot from France into Spain. Caught in an unexpected whiteout snowstorm, each step through the knee-deep snow felt like the last I could take, but if we stopped for even a minute we would most likely die in the remote, isolated place of our rest. And again, days later, I sought the answers as I stood atop Alto de Perdón, the Mount of Forgiveness, to the west of Pamplona where metal sculptures stand, representing the pilgrimages of thousands over a millennium on the Camino de Santiago.

Now as Max nears the completion of his time in the Marine Corps, service that has taken him to Europe, Asia, and Africa, we talk and dream about future endeavors. I imagine that we'll hike across Spain and explore parts of Africa together someday. I dream of returning to Kilimanjaro with Max and Eli to lead an expedition of others with challenges they seek to overcome, and for the three of us to be part of their declarations of victory at the summit. In fact, I believe that helping others to find their first summit is my calling and how I hope to make a difference for the remainder of my life.

All those years ago, before Parkinson's joined me on life's journey, I couldn't have imagined the storm I would live through or the life I now lead. Before, when I thought I was defined by education, job titles, salary, and possessions, I had never truly felt comfortable in my own skin. Then God sent Parkinson's. It forced me to grow and was the tool He used to bend, break, and reshape me into who I am meant to be. Over the years, it has been both alternately and collectively my monster, my tormenter, my prison, my teacher and, eventually, the constant companion that helps guide me on the narrow path I must follow. One thing Parkinson's will never be, though, is the victor. When I was the man I used to be, I couldn't have imagined living for years as a crippled man, only to be rebuilt and redeemed, and given the heart of a servant.

For much of my life, I had never lived fully, always holding some part of myself in reserve for protection or as an escape route if things went sideways. Everything changed the night, while on my knees, I pleaded with God to hear me and to spare my son's life. I was finally willing to surrender the last part of myself to God, and that act of depending completely on faith freed me. I was all in. I was finally ready to do whatever God wanted me to do and to go wherever He wanted me to go. He told me to get up and walk, so I got up and walked. Those steps played a part in healing my family, and eventually led me to Kilimanjaro. Seeking its summit was the step by step process of God teaching me about being all in, about the living out of commitment and faith. It was the training ground and the final exam. After reaching the top of the tallest free-standing mountain on earth, nothing seems impossible.

Sometimes I marvel at the crazy, incomprehensible life I have lived and the things I've been led to do. But I also know that I don't need to climb mountains, or run races, or make pilgrimages to be near God. He shows me He's near in simple, subtle ways every day.

One recent happening stands out. It was just an ordinary day. I woke before dawn, as is often the case, and began the day in the basement watching TV and drinking coffee. I heard a noise outside the window: It was the sound of something trapped in the deep window well. I suspected that I knew what it was even before daylight came. A baby rabbit had fallen through the grating that prevents all but the smallest of creatures from falling to the ground four feet below. There was no escape on his own. He would need my help if he was to survive.

In the rain and the glow of early morning, I removed the grate and slowly lowered the ladder down. With gloved hands, as to not leave my scent on him, I gathered him up. Then I raised my arms and when I opened my hands, he was set free. Standing there in the rain, in the limited light, in the confined space of the window well, I remembered. I remembered what Jesus did for me, and I remembered all those He sent to gather me up in the midst of the darkness, raise me up, and set me free with their unconditional love. I remembered just how fortunate I am to be living the second chance.

ACKNOWLEDGEMENTS

I want to thank all those who played a part in the creation of this book. From helping with some of the most tedious tasks to offering priceless encouragement along the way, it wouldn't exist without their help.

I am nothing if not a husband and a father. My wife and sons have kept me tethered to life in the most tenuous of circumstances and have always inspired me to be my best self. Thank you for partaking in the creation of this book. From imagining its existence with me when it was a far off dream to discussing the most minute details to offering blisteringly honest feedback, I couldn't have done it without you. I love you.

I am also a son and a brother. My mom and brothers are some of the toughest people I know. I can't imagine life without their love, encouragement, and belief in me for all of my life. Thank you for always dreaming with me. Thank you, Pete, for unofficially adopting me as your son all those years ago. Although we do not share the same blood, you have been everything a son could have wanted and needed a father to be. I can only imagine the dark paths I could have taken had it not been for your (sometimes tough) love and mentoring.

I am very grateful for the brothers and sisters I have acquired throughout my life. I have been blessed with some incredibly deep friendships. You know who you are. If you ever need me--no matter the hour, the place, or the fight--I'll be there at your side

I am indebted to Anthony P. Nicholas, M.D., Ph.D., University of Alabama at Birmingham School of Medicine, Department of Neurology: an outstanding physician, a tenacious patient advocate, and a great man. Thanks, Doc, for being my guide since PD joined me on life's journey.

I am grateful for the encouragement and expertise of my friend and editor, Laurie Knight. You helped me find my voice.

I am thankful that a group of strangers could meet in Africa, and through the sharing of incredible, life-changing experiences on Kilimanjaro, become friends and teammates for life. We will always be connected. *Asante* for your contributions to this book.

Lastly, I'd like to thank Michael J. Fox and all those who work at The Michael J. Fox Foundation for Parkinson's Research for the work they do to find the cure, and for giving me the opportunity to take a hike to the top of Africa, where I was able to declare my victory over Parkinson's.

REFERENCES

13ers.com. (2015, May 30). *The Colorado 13ers.* Retrieved from the 13ers.com website: http://www.13ers.com/peaks/13ers_all.php?displaytype=1&sublist=13ers&listd=list

14ers.com. (2015, May 30). *Colorado 14ers.* Retrieved from the 14ers.com website: http://www.14ers.com/photos/photos_14ers1.php

AlanArnett.com. (2015, May 30). *Everest Base Camp Trek FAQ.* Retrieved from website: http://www.alanarnette.com/everest/ebcfaq.php

Bataan Memorial Death March. (2015, May 27). *History of the Bataan Death March.* Retrieved from the Bataan Memorial Death March website: http://www.bataanmarch.com/r09/history.htm

Charity Navigator. (2015, May 27). *Michael J. Fox Foundation for Parkinson's Research.* Retrieved from the Charity Navigator website: http:/www.charitynavigator.org/index.cfm?bay=search.summary&orgid=7597#.VWW_6xcy_oI

Charity Watch. (2015, May 27). *Michael J. Fox Foundation for Parkinson's Research.* Retrieved from the Charity Watch website: https://www.charitywatch.org/ratings-and-metrics/michael-j-fox-foundation-for-parkinsons-research/320

Climb Kilimanjaro Guide. (2015, May 30). *Acclimatization and Altitude Sickness on Kilimanjaro.* Retrieved from the Climb Kilimanjaro Guide website: http://www.climbkilimanjaroguide.com/acclimatization-kilimanjaro/#altitude-sickness

Climb Kilimanjaro Guide. (2015, May 30). *Mount Kilimanjaro Facts.* Retrieved from the Climb Kilimanjaro Guide website: http://www.climbkilimanjaroguide.com/kilimanjaro-facts/#trekkers

Fox, M.J. (2010). *A funny thing happened on the way to the future: Twists and turns and lessons learned.* New York, NY: Hyperion.

Fox, M.J. (2002). *Lucky man: A memoir.* New York, NY: Hyperion.

Government Printing Office. (1999, September 28). Statement of Michael J. Fox, actor (p. 12). *Parkinson's disease research and treatment: Hearing before a subcommittee of the committee on appropriations United States Senate One Hundred Sixth Congress first session special hearing.* Retrieved from the Government Printing Office website: http://www.gpo.gov/fdsys/pkg/CHRG-106shrg59959/html/CHRG-106shrg59959.htm

Hemingway, E. (2007). The snows of Kilimanjaro. *The complete short stories of Ernest Hemingway: The Finca Vigía edition* (pp. 39-56). [Kindle DX version]. Retrieved from Amazon.com.

Kübler-Ross, E. (1969). *On death and dying.* New York, NY: Macmillan.

Moore, T.J., Glenmullen, J., & Mattison, D.R. (2014). Reports of pathological gambling, hypersexuality, and compulsive shopping associated with dopamine receptor agonist drugs. *JAMA Internal Medicine*, 174(12), 1930-1933. doi:10.1001/jamainternmed.2014.5262.

National Park Service (2015, May 27). *Great Smoky Mountains: History of Cades Cove*. Retrieved from the National Park Service website: http://www.nps.gov/grsm/learn/historyculture/cades-cove-history.htm

National Park Service (2015, May 27). *Great Smoky Mountains: Park Statistics*. Retrieved from the National Park Service website: http://www.nps.gov/grsm/learn/management/statistics.htm

National Parkinson Foundation. (2015, May 27). *Young-Onset Parkinson's*. Retrieved from the National Parkinson Foundation website:http://www.parkinson.org/Parkinson-s-Disease/Young-Onset-Parkinsons

Parkinson's Disease Foundation. (2015, May 27). *What is Parkinson's disease?* Retrieved from the Parkinson's Disease Foundation website: http://www.pdf.org/about_pd

Reuters. (2014, January 31). *Tech Videos: Laser technology lets Parkinsonism patients walk again*. Retrieved from the Reuters website: http://www.reuters.com/video/2015/04/15/laser-technology-lets-parkinsonism-patie?videoId=276660489

Sledge, E. (2007). *With the Old Breed at Peleliu and Okinawa* (Presidio Press trade pbk. ed.). New York: Presidio Press.

Stedman, H. (2010). *Kilimanjaro: The trekking guide to Africa's highest mountain* (3rd ed.). Hindhead: Trailblazer.

The Michael J. Fox Foundation for Parkinson's Research. (2015, May 27). *Dystonia and Parkinson's disease.* Retrieved from the Michael J. Fox Foundation website: https://www. michaeljfox.org/understanding-parkinsons/living-with-pd/ topic.php?dystonia

The Michael J. Fox Foundation for Parkinson's Research. (2015, May 27). *Financials.* Retrieved from the Michael J. Fox Foundation website: https://www.michaeljfox.org/page. html?foundation-financials

The Michael J. Fox Foundation for Parkinson's Research. (2012, October 3). *Foxfeed Blog: Debi Brooks' First Day on the Job, Twelve Years Later: Still "Fully Energized by the Possibilities."* Retrieved from the Michael J. Fox Foundation website: https://www.michaeljfox.org/foundation/news-detail. php?debi-brooks-first-day-job

The Michael J. Fox Foundation for Parkinson's Research. (2012, February 1). *Foxfeed Blog: Summit Mt. Kilimanjaro: Join Team Fox on an Expedition to Reach the Top of Africa.* Retrieved from the Michael J. Fox Foundation website: https://www. michaeljfox.org/foundation/news-detail.php?Summit-Mt-Kilimanjaro:-Join-Team-Fox-on-an-Expedition-to-Reach-the-Top-of-Africa

The Michael J. Fox Foundation for Parkinson's Research. (2015, May 27). *Get Involved.* Retrieved from the Michael J. Fox Foundation website: https://www.michaeljfox.org/get-involved/teamfox.php

The Michael J. Fox Foundation for Parkinson's Research. (2015, May 27). *Participate In Parkinson's Research.* Retrieved from the Michael J. Fox Foundation website: https://www.michaeljfox.org/page.html?Participate-in-Parkinsons-Research

ABOUT THE AUTHOR

Diagnosed with Parkinson's disease in his mid-thirties, R.W. Long spent years learning how to live in a body that wouldn't cooperate. Motivated by the love of his family and driven by his faith in God, he was able to forge a new life of unlimited possibilities. Long, the father of two Marines, lives in Colorado with his wife and dog. Spending time with family, climbing mountains, training for endurance events, and seeking ways to help others find their first summit are his passions.

For more information, please visit www.firstsummitproject.org

Made in the USA
Monee, IL
07 April 2021